Behavioral Safety

A Framework for Success

Dominic Cooper Ph.D.

Co-founder & CEO

B-Safe Management Solutions, Inc.

Published by

BSMS

www.bsms-inc.com   www.b-safe.net   www.behavioral-safety.com

Library of Congress Control Number: 2009908845

ISBN 978-0-9842039-0-1

Printed in the United States of America

Behavioral Safety

A Framework for Success

About the Author

Dominic Cooper, Ph.D. is one of the world's leading authorities in Behavioral Safety.

Dr. Cooper is both a Business Psychologist and a Safety Professional who has implemented behavior-based processes internationally for over 20 years. A past Professor at Indiana University, he has written 5 books and over 150 articles on Behavioral Safety, Safety Culture change, and Safety Leadership.

More than an academic, Dr. Cooper has worked shoulder-to-shoulder, on-site with frontline managers and employees, creating and fine-tuning the most effective Behavioral Safety process available. As the CEO of his behavioral consulting firm B-Safe Management Solutions, Dr. Cooper is actively engaged with clients, is a well-known speaker, and is a member of several professional organizations.

Dr. Cooper developed B-Safe®, an award winning Behavioral Safety process, and he co-founded BSMS Inc, an international behavior-based safety consulting firm operating in the Americas, Asia, Africa, Australasia, Europe, and the Middle East. His clients consistently achieve world-class safety performance.

Dr. Cooper continues to innovate and refine his process by actively working as an on-site consultant and project manager. He maintains his grounding in real-world safety issues by participating in, and managing, multi-consultant, multi-site projects on Behavioral Safety, Safety Culture improvement, and Safety Leadership.

Contents

Foreword

I have long been an admirer of Dom Cooper's work, first as a researcher and a practitioner, now as an author. Dom's unique perspective is anchored in his experiences as a scaffolder in the construction industry. The avoidable injuries he witnessed on the job encouraged him to enter the university and study to become a safety professional.

Dom's advanced degrees in industrial psychology, his safety knowledge, and his thorough grounding in frontline job safety issues make him one of the most credible behavioral safety authorities in the world. His unique background allows him to contribute a richer understanding of safety culture to the field of behavioral safety.

Those who understand safety culture as Dom does, understand that leadership practices functionally define the safety culture of an organization. Dom talks about safety leadership practices more precisely than most of the other established behavioral safety experts.

One of the strengths of this book is that it clearly explains that behavioral safety is implemented in different ways within different companies, cultures, and regions of the world. While Dom and I have different strategies for implementing behavioral safety, this book presents the strengths of Dom's approach in a practical and understandable way. Anyone reading Dom's book will quickly know why he is acknowledged as one of the world's leading authorities in behavioral safety.

Dom has extensive experience implementing behavior-based safety with clients worldwide. This book incorporates the experience and wisdom he acquired while adapting behavioral safety to such diverse areas as Sub-Saharan Africa, the Middle East, Europe, and the Far East. The reader is provided with insights about how Dom's practical approach was successfully adapted to the culture of those organizations and countries.

In short, I learned a lot about our craft from reading this book. You will too. Dom has written this book for people to read, not for the shelves of academics.

If you are just learning about behavioral safety, if you work in a company that has a behavior-based safety process, if you provide behavior-based safety services, if it is something you are involved with, or if it is just something you are interested in --- buy this book.

You will come away from it with a better understanding of behavior-based safety and its adaptability to a wide variety of cultures and settings.

Terry E. McSween, Ph.D.

President and CEO of Quality Safety Edge

Preface

I have written this book with a straightforward purpose in mind: to provide readers with a practical route map to help build and sustain a high quality Behavioral Safety process regardless of industry, country, or culture. The deliberate use of the word 'framework' in the book title conveys the essence of the repeated lesson learned throughout my working life as a soldier, scaffolder, safety specialist, scholar, and scribe: provide structure. Without structure to provide the 'backbone' any improvement effort is doomed to failure, particularly in the world of work. An examination of why so many Behavioral Safety processes have failed to live up to their promises can be ascribed to a failure to optimally configure its structure. In turn, this has often led to a lack of focus, purpose, and execution as people are not clear about what they should do and when they should do it. Similarly the use of the word 'success' in the title is based on what I have seen and experienced in my 20-year journey in the Behavioral Safety arena in a multitude of industries and settings. Although there are many definitions of what success means, to me, the primary success factor is that an injury or catastrophe has been avoided as a result of a concerted proactive effort, based on a genuine safety partnership between management and the workforce.

Behavioral Safety is based on three traditions: safety science, psychology, and management. Safety science has taught us the extreme importance of management's commitment to safety and their safety leadership. Psychology has taught us why people behave the way they do and how the work environment and managerial systems exert powerful influences on people's behavior. Management science and practice has taught us that a systematic and focused continual improvement effort is required if we are to achieve our objectives. Optimal Behavioral Safety processes recognize the strong inter-relationships between these three disciplines and strive to incorporate them to create a focused 'safety partnership' that is so vital for success.

Behavioral Safety has now become an established cost-effective weapon in the war on workplace injuries. As a direct consequence of the approach, many companies around the world have reduced their injury rates, while simultaneously improving their efficiency, reliability, quality, competitiveness, and profitability.

This book is intended for those who wish to know what is involved in developing, executing, and maintaining a Behavioral Safety process. The content presents an integrated approach known to work in all types of settings to deliver world-class safety performance. It is not intended to be a 'cookbook' containing the perfect recipe, but is rather a guide to the most important issues that need to be considered at each stage, based on what is currently known. I have drawn from a wide variety of sources to present the latest thinking and knowledge on the topic. I have also tried to highlight best practice throughout, which is reflected in the Behavioral Safety Maturity Ladder presented in chapter 2. In essence the Behavioral Safety Maturity Ladder represents a continuum reflecting increasing levels of involvement, coverage, and use of leading indicators. Its purpose is to assist companies to establish their current level of Behavioral Safety maturity and identify the actions required to achieve excellence. Whether you're just beginning or already have a process in operation, the Maturity Model can be used as a guide to 'aim for the stars' from the start, or can help to identify 'areas of opportunity' to improve.

In this book I attempt to answer many of the questions surrounding Behavioral Safety in plain, everyday language. It starts with the business case, highlights the lessons learned over the past 30 years or so, outlines important implementation principles, and then takes the reader on a step-by-step process of assessment, development, rollout, and maintenance. This culminates in special considerations for large scale or short-term implementations and the presentation of sample case histories. I trust readers will find it a useful reference source for their improvement efforts.

Dominic Cooper
August 2009

Acknowledgments

The phrase *'We stand on the shoulders of giants'* is certainly true in my case. I have been extremely fortunate over the years to have had the opportunity to study with the world's best. Ivan T Robertson (Professor Emeritus of Work and Organizational Psychology at Manchester University) had a particularly profound influence on my professional development. Always encouraging, but a stickler for the facts, he taught me what it means to be a scientific researcher and a writer. The works of earlier and contemporary Behavioral Safety scholars and practitioners have also taught me the value of keeping an open mind. There are a vast range of approaches that these people have expanded upon to enlighten me in my quest and thirst for knowledge. Professional colleagues and industry clients, particularly those in the Oil & Gas sector, have also helped to stretch and polish my knowledge to the point where I feel it would be valuable to pass this on to others in book form.

I am deeply indebted to, and appreciative of, the many people who have assisted me in writing this book. Jerry Pounds, Senior Vice President of Quality Safety Edge has been an absolute star. His keen insights have helped keep the book focused and on track and kept me away from academic language. Even though they are very busy, the staff at SABIC Petrochemicals (UK) Ltd have been brilliant at pointing out the errors of my ways with some of the chapters. My family and friends have also helped by correcting my bad grammar and pointing out paragraphs and concepts that I made difficult for them to understand. My wife and partner, Gerry, has been truly amazing. She has read every word, re-created some of the graphics, designed the book cover and taken care of all the administrative aspects.

They say that behind every successful man, there is a good woman. Not a truer word can be said about my wife. Since the day I came home from a day's scaffolding work and told Gerry I wanted to go to college, she has offered her total, undying support. This has meant considerable sacrifice on her part over the years. I flitted in and out of home doing my thing while she raised our children almost single-handedly. I am eternally beholden to her and love her deeply.

1 Why Everyone Is Implementing Behavioral Safety

After two hours of torrential rain, Ted and the guys went back to work. They were erecting scaffolding on the gable end of the North wall on a Nuclear Power Station build. The project was behind schedule and a lot of pressure, underpinned by contract penalties, was being exerted on the guys to 'catch-up'. Ted climbed up one of the uprights on the outside of the scaffold to reach his workplace, while shouting instructions to his crew to fetch the materials he wanted. The system scaffolding being used was painted and varnished, and with the rain it had become slippery. Ted never got to his workplace. He fell and landed on the steel reinforcing bars poking out of the concrete, which pierced his body in numerous places. His crew sounded the alarm. The site's emergency procedures were put into effect. One of the crane operators tried lowering a 'stretcher' to where Ted had landed, but it could not reach. Word quickly spread to all the scaffolders on site that one of 'theirs' had gone down, that he was still alive, but the stretcher could not reach him. The entire site population consisting of 5000 people stopped working as forty-five scaffolders tunneled their way through the dense two-hundred foot mass of scaffolding built over the previous 6 months to reach him. This took over 3 hours, during which time Ted passed over to the other side.

So what triggered this incident? Well, depending on your viewpoint there are a number of circumstances: [1] work was behind schedule, so people were trying to play catch up; [2] Ted climbed up the outside of the scaffold instead of using the ladders that were available (he had even put some of them in place!); [3] the site's emergency procedures did not work (they had not been tested in this spot); and, [4] it had rained, making everything wet and slippery.

The single issue that would have prevented the incident was Ted using the ladders instead of climbing up the outside of the scaffold. In other words, if Ted had behaved safely, he would be alive today. In line with modern theories of accident causation, a multitude of factors were at play, that in combination caused [1] the unnecessary death of a decent, honest, hard-working family man; [2] a major loss in site productivity; and [3] significant amounts of rework to replace the scaffolding removed when trying to reach Ted.

What could have influenced Ted to climb to his workplace safely, using the ladders? Simple! His crewmembers could have intervened and steered him away from his intended actions. Many of us informally do so every single day with our family, friends and colleagues to keep them safe. At work, when this exact same process is formalized, and systematically applied, it is termed Behavior-Based Safety (BBS) or Behavioral Safety.

Benefits

The benefits of a person intervening when someone is in danger of hurting themselves or others are obvious. But imagine how the safety and business performance of your company could be improved if this was done on a larger scale. Evidence from numerous real-life Behavioral Safety case histories and scientific research studies shows us what is possible.

In Chicago, Amtrak reduced their injury rates by 80 percent within 12 months, and saved $300,000 per year. Similarly, over an 18-month period, RasGas, a major Oil & Gas company, achieved a staggering 136 million man-hours without a lost-time accident to become the safest upstream Oil & Gas Company in the world, two years running. SABIC Olefins reduced both lost-time and recordable injuries, saved $500,000 per year in steam leaks through identifying and making repairs, achieved a 32% reduction in insurance premiums, and significantly reduced operating costs as workers identified and rectified plant problems themselves.

Paul Booth, President of SABIC UK Petrochemicals stated *'behavioral-safety has brought about a fundamental shift in attitude towards Safety, Health and Environment. It has for the first time allowed every individual in the business to personally take responsibility for their own safety and for the safety of others'*.

CITGO Petroleum (Refining) was best in class in refining in the US from 2003-2008, while simultaneously achieving an 88% reduction in worker's compensation claims and 96% reduction in workers compensation costs from their Behavioral Safety process. Foster Wheeler, a global engineering and construction company, examined the safety-productivity link and found an overlap of 63 percent. When safety improved, productivity also improved by an average of 12 percent. As these examples show, *good Behavioral Safety processes are good business.* They reduce injuries and improve the 'bottom-line'.

A Brief History

Behavioral Safety is derived from a rich application history of behavioral approaches in a wide variety of work settings, extending back over the past five decades. These began in earnest during the 1960's. Companies such as Emery Air Freight, AT&T, GE, and General Motors established training and productivity programs. These targeted key performance areas such as quality, cost control, error rates, and absenteeism, and produced stunning results.

Perhaps one of the most powerful long-term demonstrations is that of Milliken & Company, headquartered in South Carolina. Since the early 1980's this company has adopted behavioral principles, and has received numerous prestigious quality awards. It was also voted as one of *'The 17 Safest Companies in America'* and as one of the top four companies in the Nation for OSHA Voluntary Protection Program (VPP) STAR sites (all of Milliken's U.S. manufacturing operations are OSHA STAR certified).

The first formal Behavioral Safety study was in 1960 – it focused on the behavior of hooking back chains in walkways. This study placed posters at key locations in the plant, and the frequency with which people complied with the message was counted. This study proved safety behavior could be changed relatively simply via focused interventions. Throughout the 1960's and 1970's many scholars and practitioners began to write about the application of behavioral principles for a wider audience. The mid 1970's saw the 'real' beginnings of the fledgling Behavioral Safety movement with great success in coalmines, fabrication plants, and public work departments.

A steady stream of academic studies followed throughout the 1980's, conducted in the Manufacturing, Health Care, Foods and Oil, and Gas sectors. In parallel, commercialization of the approach began in the US that continued to achieve astonishing results. In the late 1980's, early 1990's, scientific studies were being conducted in Europe, primarily in construction and shipbuilding that achieved similar results indicating the approach is universally applicable regardless of culture. At the present time, Behavioral Safety has been adopted in Africa, Asia, Australasia, the Middle East and South America in numerous industries, and is now a worldwide phenomenon.

The names of companies spearheading Behavioral Safety are too numerous to mention, but many are in the Fortune 500. In other words, they are household names covering a wide range of industries that includes Aviation, Agrichemicals, Chemicals, Health Care, Logging, Mining, Nuclear Energy, Oil & Gas, Paper, Petrochemicals, Pharmaceuticals, Retail Sales, Steel, Transport, and Utilities.

The spread of Behavioral Safety is perhaps largely due to [1] insurers requiring or urging clients to adopt it; [2] multi-nationals requiring their sub-contractors and suppliers to implement it; and, [3] encouragement from national HSE regulators, based on the typical results achieved. Aside from reducing injuries, other motives for using Behavioral Safety include wanting to be 'Best in Class', wanting to involve employees in the safety effort, wanting to mesh safety into a QMS framework, wanting to gain 'competitive advantage', or, all of the above.

What is Behavioral Safety?

The purpose of a Behavioral Safety process is to reduce incidents triggered by 'unsafe' behaviors. To achieve this, Behavioral Safety processes locate specific behavioral problems by focusing on incidents resulting from the interaction between people and their wider working environment. This includes the presence, quality, and functioning of various management systems (safety and non-safety), the quality of leadership, the resources available (financial and non-financial), and the overall safety culture.

Once identified, attempts are made to discover the triggers (e.g. unavailable equipment) driving unsafe behavior (e.g. using improvised tools), and what factors are maintaining the unsafe behavior (e.g. getting the job done), so appropriate corrective actions can be taken.

Executing the change strategy usually involves addressing the triggers to remove inappropriate 'drivers' and establishing a monitoring process to help improve the frequency of the desired safe behaviors. The results are used to facilitate feedback, appropriate corrective actions (e.g. remove hazardous materials, etc), and the tracking of progress. Data trends are used to adapt the process to suit the particular circumstances (e.g. shift the focus to other behaviors).

Behavioral Safety has been defined as *the application of behavioral research on human performance to the problems of safety in the workplace*. Written by academics, broad definitions such as this, fail to inform users of what it actually is and what it means. A good definition should be constructed in the same way as a good vision statement, spelling out the direction and actions a company wishes to pursue. In a more practical vein, therefore, my definition of Behavioral Safety is:

'A process that creates a *safety partnership* between management and the workforce by continually focusing everyone's attention and actions on their own, and others, safety behavior'.

This definition communicates the dynamic and adaptive nature of Behavioral Safety, what it tries to achieve, and the actions required to get there. Behavioral Safety is a dynamic process with specific program elements. Together these comprise a continual improvement process. This can be clearly seen in Exhibit 1.1.

Exhibit 1.1: Behavioral Safety Process Cycle

The process starts with briefings to stakeholders, and potentially, a Cultural Assessment. Training project team members to drive the process, which then facilitates checklist development, managerial alignment, observer training, measurement, goal setting, feedback, and corrective actions, follows this. At future intervals, the entire process is reviewed and adapted to suit any changed circumstances.

You might ask, 'Why is the creation of a safety partnership important'? Evidence-based research and practical everyday experience tells us that good safety performance does not come about from management alone (This includes senior, middle, and front-line). In most instances, management's role is to provide strategic direction, leadership, and the necessary resources. In other words, managers facilitate people's needs to enable them to get their job done safely and efficiently. By and large, within the constraints imposed on them by leadership and external market conditions, many managers do these things.

Equally, frontline employees cannot deliver good safety performance alone. They rely on management providing a safe working environment, effective safety management systems and procedures, the right tools and equipment, and sufficient time to do their jobs safely and efficiently. When all these aspects have been attended to, people tend to work safely 100 percent of the time. As such, it is logical that companies can only achieve good safety performance when everyone works together to achieve the common goal of zero injuries. In essence this means effective safety must be a partnership.

Paul Leigh, a Professor of Health Economics at the University of California conservatively estimated 2005 work-related injuries cost the US $115.1 Billion. In 2004 the average *direct cost* of one lost-time incident (i.e. an injured person was away from the workplace until they had recovered) was $28,000. OSHA also estimates *indirect costs* are ten times the direct costs. Companies, therefore, can be expected to spend an average $308,000 per lost-time injury.

If a company's profit margin were ten percent, $3,080,000 would have to be invested to be able to afford just one lost-time injury. Since 'an ounce of prevention is worth a pound of cure', a genuine safety partnership flowing from a Behavioral Safety process will help to significantly reduce injuries and their associated costs. The benefits could also spill over into quality, production and environmental performance that can only be for the common good.

The Behavior - Incident Relationship

Various studies have put numbers to different categories of injury outcome and these are usually referred to as 'accident triangles' (see Exhibit 1.2). Although the numbers may differ, these illustrate that as severity decreases frequency increases.

Exhibit 1.2: Accident Triangle

It is often a matter of chance whether 'low severity' incidents such as 'near-hits' (others use the term near-miss), become events with more serious consequences. Thus, the severity of outcome cannot be controlled. *Preventative opportunities* arise, therefore, from controlling unsafe acts, unsafe conditions, and system faults at the base of the accident triangle. If action can be taken at this level, the chances of more serious injuries occurring will be greatly reduced.

One of Behavioral Safety's main objectives is to help people address the unsafe behaviors and/or the unsafe conditions and system faults at the bottom of the triangle. By reducing the number of these hazards at the bottom of the triangle we also correspondingly reduce the opportunity for injuries, and in the worst case – fatalities. Behavioral Safety is a proactive method for preventing hazards from escalating into incidents and injuries.

The evidence overwhelmingly shows incident reductions when Behavioral Safety processes are introduced and maintained. Exhibit 1.3 lists ten common approaches to improving safety performance obtained from 53 research articles. Ranked according to the mean percentage decrease in injury rates, it shows both behavioral and ergonomic approaches lead by a substantial margin.

Behavioral Safety advocates applaud the valuable contribution other approaches make to improving safety. Anything that reduces injuries is good. Activities such as engineering changes, group-problem solving, management audits and information campaigns (i.e. safety posters) have all been shown to exert a clear impact. Combining and using *all* the approaches shown in Exhibit 1.3 will exert an enormous influence. The study does highlight, however, that as one component of an overall approach to reducing injuries, Behavioral Safety can play an extremely important role.

Approach	Number of Studies	Number of Subjects	Average Reduction
1. Behavioral-based	7	2444	59.6%
2. Ergonomics	3	Unknown	51.6%
3. Engineering change	4	Unknown	29.0%
4. Group Problem Solving	1	76	20.0%
5. Government Action	2	Unknown	18.3%
6. Management Audits	4	Unknown	17.0%
7. Stress Management	2	1300	15.0%
8. Poster Campaign	2	6100	14.0%
9. Personnel Selection	26	19177	3.7%
10. Near-Miss Reporting	2	Unknown	0.0%

Exhibit 1.3: Comparison of Approaches to Reduce Work Injuries

Two Sides of the Same Coin

Companies are run by businessmen who adopt performance improvement initiatives *proven* to deliver tangible business benefits. Quality Management Systems (QMS) linking product and service quality to customer satisfaction provide one clear example. In essence, QMS and its variants (Six Sigma, Lean Manufacturing) are concerned with continual quality improvement resulting in better business performance and profitability. Six-Sigma has been defined as:

'An organized and systematic method for strategic process improvement and new product and service development that relies on statistical methods and the scientific method to make dramatic reductions in customer defined defect rates.'

Behavioral Safety achieves better safety performance and reduces costs (adding to profitability) with similar strategies and methods, except it maintains a continual focus on safety improvement. Both use a *'define, measure, analyze, improve and control'* process model, based on Deming's 'Plan-Do-Check-Act' cycle. Behavioral Safety, therefore, is nothing more or less than a component of a company's safety management system requiring a concerted, focused effort to produce the desired results. The simple five-step management model adopted by most Behavioral Safety processes, outlined below, makes CLEAR the parallels with Quality Management.

1. **C**larify the objectives
2. **L**ocate the problems
3. **E**xecute the change strategy
4. **A**ssess current progress
5. **R**eview and adapt the process.

Behavioral Safety also makes use of 80/20 thinking, which is a principle based on the notion that 80 percent of consequences arise from 20 percent of causes. The trick is to be selective and identify the 20 percent of incident causes that will eliminate 80 percent of them. Once achieved it is time to move on to address the next 20 percent of incident causes, and so on. In this way, provided 'we stay in lane', incidents can be entirely eliminated over a relatively short time period.

QMS and Behavioral Safety, therefore, represent two sides of the same coin – both use data to inform decision-making. Both also identify predictors of performance so they can be defined and measured. In the case of Behavioral Safety these predictors are obtained from an analysis of existing incident records so as to target the small proportion of behaviors triggering the lion's share of the incidents. Once measured the data is analyzed to identify trends to ascertain improvements and provide feedback to assist in problem solving.

Typically, QMS uses Statistical Process Control (SPC) techniques to monitor fluctuations in performance trends. Any changes resulting from corrective actions are assessed to ensure breakthroughs are genuine. In safety management, it is also common for companies to focus on incident rates ((number of incidents X 200,000)/number of hours worked) as the primary 'lagging' indicator of safety performance. Some companies analyze these with SPC techniques to determine whether a company's safety performance is really improving, getting worse, or whether the performance fluctuations are simply due to chance. Performance is worsening, if the incident rate climbs through the upper limits. Performance is genuinely getting better if it slices through the lower limits. In between, means performance is broadly staying the same.

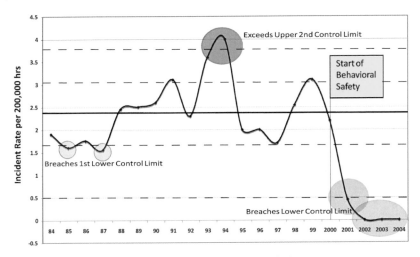

Exhibit 1.4: Incident Rate Variation

This can be clearly seen in Exhibit 1.4, which presents 'real' incident data over a 21-year period. For the first eight years, average safety performance broadly stayed the same. We can see the incident rate worsened in 1993/4, got better in 1995/6/7 but rose again in 1998/99. The reasons for this 'roller coaster ride' in performance can be many and varied, but usually indicates safety is being 'managed by exception'. This means that when immediate problems appear to be resolved, management attention and resources are diverted to other pressing organizational issues until such time as incident rates rise again. As a whole the incident rates between 1984 and 2000 appeared to have hit a 'plateau' with performance being relatively stable. Obviously, something new was required to make the step change.

A good example of a safety partnership, a joint management & employee team reviewed every aspect of the way safety was being managed. One of the conclusions was to introduce Behavioral Safety across the site, which was introduced in late fall of 2000. By the end of 2001, the incident rate was just inside the lower limit, with performance slicing through in 2002/3/4, indicating genuine performance improvements. The cause in this instance was the introduction of a new phenomenon: Behavioral Safety.

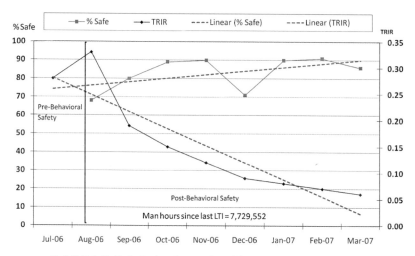

Exhibit 1.5: Safe Behavior and Incident Rate Relationship

Good Behavioral Safety processes also trend a wide range of 'leading' indicator measurements focused on process issues such as the percent safe score, participation rates, and corrective action rates. An example from construction, shown in Exhibit 1.5, reveals that as targeted safety behaviors improve, the incident rate correspondingly reduces. Clearly, therefore, Behavioral Safety processes provide a useful means to measure and control ongoing safety performance. It does so by linking continual improvement in safety behavior with reduced incident rates to deliver tangible business benefits, which primarily are in the form of reduced human capital and financial costs. The safety behavior levels tend to be expressed as the Percent Safe score (i.e. the ratio between safe and unsafe behaviors). Good Behavioral Safety processes also focus on 'lagging' outcomes such as incident rates to provide a validation check that the process measures are correctly targeting the areas of concern, and addressing the problem.

Adopting Behavioral Safety

Companies most likely to adopt Behavioral Safety are those that have been through two previous safety management approaches: Engineering and Procedural. An engineering approach attempts to improve safe performance by 'engineering' or designing out hazards. In other words, designing better and safer equipment, installing physical barriers (e.g. machine guards), changing the physical working environment so that it is safe, and making use of Preventative Maintenance schedules to keep machinery and equipment in a safe condition should stop some incidents occurring. As shown in Exhibit 1.3, the average impact is about a 29 percent reduction.

Procedural approaches refer to the development of policies, procedures, and rules for every task. Both the legislature and the company management set the tone of these to ensure compliance. In general, policies are set for every aspect of safety by the company's most senior management at board level. These are further expanded upon by local business unit managers in the context of their sphere of operations. The policies tend to lead to procedural reviews within a particular function (e.g. Production, Engineering, and Procurement). In turn these lead to the development of rules that codify how particular tasks must be performed safely. 'Risk Assessments' or Job Safety Analyses of one sort or another, underpin the whole process.

The results of these approaches tend to lead to incremental improvements in incident rates over a number of years. Despite their best efforts, however, companies often reach a 'plateau' beyond which the incident rate does not seem to decrease. When they examine their incident records, most appear to be triggered by unsafe behavior. Those unaware of the impact that Behavioral Safety can exert, will often develop more rules and procedures in an effort to bring the identified behaviors under control. In other words, they continue to do the same things, but with increased intensity.

Unfortunately, it is virtually impossible to codify every aspect of behavior within any given set of procedures. Even if this were possible, people would still have to follow them. Ted, for example, knew climbing up the outside of the scaffold was contrary to the rules and procedures, but he did it anyway. Thus, increasing the numbers of procedures inevitably requires a greater degree of management time to ensure compliance.

Management time is one of the most precious commodities in business, and spending it to 'police' compliance to additional procedures rather than focusing on the core activities that will increase profits seems a pointless exercise. Behavioral Safety processes overcome this management time issue by involving everyone in the safety effort, thereby distributing responsibility for safety to all. If done properly, it also helps identify 'opportunities for change' in the quality, reliability and effectiveness of management systems to facilitate increases in competitiveness and profitability.

Summary

Based on extensive scientific research in management, safety, and psychology, Behavioral Safety processes have repeatedly been shown to deliver cost-effective business benefits in almost all industrial sectors, across the globe. The tools, methods and processes mirror those found in quality management systems, except its focus is on safety behavior rather than products and services.

In line with the maxim *'the business of business is business'*, those adopting a proactive Behavioral Safety process know it makes good economic sense to eliminate injury causing incidents and their associated costs. They also recognize benefits simultaneously spillover to enhance productivity, quality, reliability, and efficiency. In many cases, it also provides competitive advantage.

2 Lessons from Twenty Years Experience

A gas operating plant with 2000 workers conducted briefings and an assessment of safety practices with all personnel before developing and implementing Behavioral Safety. Much skepticism was revealed about management's safety practices and many unresolved safety hazards. The process was designed to include both managers and the workforce to meet the objectives of achieving a minimum 40 percent reduction in injuries, a 95 percent corrective action rate, and 95 percent managerial safety leadership exhibited within the first 12 months.

A trained project team designed the process so one member of a workgroup observed his colleagues once a day for 10-20 minutes, against an observation checklist containing very specific behaviors, for six months. The checklist would then be reviewed and adapted and another crewmember rotating into the observers role for six months, and so on. Managers developed a list of 10 safety leadership behaviors they agreed to self-monitor every week. Within four weeks different checklists had been developed for every area of operations (i.e. control room, maintenance, utilities, admin, etc). 200 observers were then trained to ensure there was an observer in every shift and plant area. All management levels went through a one-day safety leadership workshop where they were taught communication, coaching and feedback skills. Formal mini-reviews were scheduled on a quarterly basis, to help ensure the process was going to meet its objectives.

In the first six months, the incident rate reduced by 38 percent, with average safe behavior improving from 58 to 78 percent. The corrective action rate had reached 44 percent, with safely leadership running at 70 percent. A mini review identified opportunities for improvement existed in communications and the corrective action system.

By the end of the first 12 months, average safe behavior reached 94 percent; safety leadership an average 86 percent and a corrective action rate of 67 percent. The Lost-time Incident Rate plummeted by 62 percent from 0.21 to 0.08, with the Total Recordable Incident Rate reducing from 0.51 to 0.33, some 36 percent. Overall, incident rates fell by 49 percent, achieving one of the original objectives.

Although site personnel were pleased with the results to date, a formal management review of the process was conducted with the purpose of enhancing it further. This recommended efforts to be focused on improving the corrective action system and levels of safety leadership. The following year all targets were met and the site achieved a further 50 percent incident reduction.

The example outlines a well-designed and executed process. However, not every process is designed or executed in the same way, and not all achieve significant incident reductions. This highlight's the fact there are various Behavioral Safety approaches, each reflecting different degrees of maturity and effectiveness.

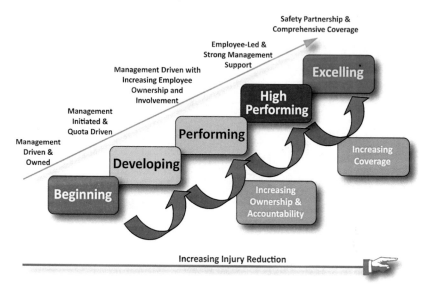

Exhibit 2.1: Behavioral Safety Maturity Ladder

The Behavioral Safety Maturity Ladder shown in Exhibit 2.1 is based on meta-analytic research examining design characteristics and their impact on incident reduction. It also reflects many practical lessons learned over the years. Its purpose is twofold: to assist companies to (a) establish their current maturity level; and (b) identify the actions required to achieve excellence. In essence the maturity ladder is a continuum that reflects increasing levels of involvement and coverage. Research has shown the greater the degree of ownership and use of leading indicators, the greater the degree of injury reduction.

Broadly comparable with the British HSE's Safety Culture Maturity Model, an 'Excelling' Behavioral Safety process is likely to correspond to high levels of Safety Culture maturity. A matrix for assessing the maturity of a Behavioral Safety process is shown in Exhibit 2.2.

Level 5, *'Excelling'* refers to a continually improving process that is owned jointly by management and employees in a safety partnership that is focused on people's specific safety-related behaviors at each level of the accident causation chain, regardless of their job function. Two-way feedback is seen as a constructive process that leads to measurable changes in the factors driving unsafe behavior or creating unsafe conditions. A wide-ranging 'basket' of leading indicators specific to the Behavioral Safety process is regularly monitored and used to highlight opportunities for change. Safety leadership is integral to the process, not a separate add-on. A Behavioral Safety specialist holds regular and frequent sustainability reviews.

Level 4, *'High Performing'* processes are largely employee-driven, with strong management support. Observations are primarily 'peer-to-peer' processes aimed at 'shop floor' employees, focused on specific categories and behaviors. There is an increased focus on the quality of observations. Data tabulations are used to guide the efforts of project teams and focus groups to eliminate 'barriers' to unsafe behavior. Safety leadership tends to be a separate process. Sustainability reviews tend to be held annually.

Level 3, *'Performing'* refers to management initiated and driven Behavioral Safety processes, where people are mandated to observe people in the workplace and complete some form of broad-based observation card. Verbal feedback tends to be provided on the spot, but data collation and analyses does not always take place. Trending is mostly focused on participation and observation rates.

Level 2, *'Developing'* processes are management initiated with 'quota' achievement being the primary driver for observations. Categories of behaviors on cards tend to be 'broad-based' or non-existent. Feedback tends to be verbal, with little attempt to tabulate data for identifying trends to remove safety problems.

Level 1, *'Beginning'* is purely management driven and owned. Ad-hoc observations are centered on the safety knowledge of the observer and have no clear focus. Observation data is not used or tabulated to drive improvements.

Criteria	Level 1 Beginning	Level 2 Developing	Level 3 Performing	Level 4 High Performing	Level 5 Excelling
Ownership	Management Driven	Management initiated & quota driven	Management driven with increasing employee involvement	Largley Employee-led Strong Management support	Management & workforce safety partnership
Sampling Tools	None	Broad Categories No definitions	Broad Categories Behaviors broadly defined	Broad Categories Specific behaviors-defined	Continual updating & review of specific behaviors. Tools cover entire accident causation chain
Training	Managerial Observation Training	Workers trained to observe	Managers & workers trained to observe & provide feedback	Managers & workers trained to observe, provide feedback & coach	Continual honing of behavioral skills for all staff
Observation Approach	Ad-hoc observations	Observation quotas	Frequent employee Peer-to-Peer Observations	Frequent management & employee Peer-to-Peer Observations	Regular Observations using a mixture of daily , workgroup. Peer-to-Peer, Outcome & self-observation approaches
Contact Rate	Ad-hoc	Monthly or quarterly, per observer	Less than once per week,per observer, but more than once per month	More than once per week, per observer	Daily safety observations. Weekly safety leadership & other supportive behaviors
Quality of Observation	No Monitoring	Focused on quota achievement	Focused solely on participation & observation rates	Increasing emphasis on quality of observations	Continually monitored & results compared with incident records
Feedback	One-way verbal feedback from manager to employees	One-way from observer to observed	Increasing two-way dialogue to identify root causes Verbal feedback only	Two-way dialogue to identify and resolve root causes of unsafe behavior Two feedback channels used	Two-way, constructive, open dialogue to identify and resolve issues and unsafe behavior More than two feedback channels provided and used, including data analysis and tabulation
Data Use	Observation data not collated	Monitoring of quota achievement only	Participation & observation rates trended Observation data recorded but not used	Observation data tabulated monthly & used by project team / focus groups to resolve issues	Tabulated data presented weekly to workgroups / managers to resolve issues at relevant level Concerted focus on on a basket leading indicators that are trended & analysed Separate Focus Groups taget salient issues
Sustainability Reviews	No reviews	Informal project team reviews	Internal management/ project team reviews	Annual independent expert reviews	Frequent independent expert sustainability reviews. Representative learning group meet monthly to discuss innovation / issues
Marketing	No Marketing	Branded process Individual rewards / recognition	Branded process with widely available promotional materials Individual rewards / recognition	Branded process with widely available promotional materials Regular achievement celebrations Individual rewards / recognition	Branded process with widely available promotional materials Regular achievement celebrations Regular monthly newsletters Team rewards / recognition Annual Performance Appraisals dependent on safety leadership exhibited

Exhibit 2.2: Behavioral Safety Maturity Matrix

When a multi-national petrochemical company assessed various forms of Behavioral Safety processes across three European countries, a similar maturity ladder proved extremely useful for highlighting improvement opportunities. It also helped to identify the evolutionary stage reached by each particular approach.

This can be seen in Exhibit 2.3, where the first profile was assessed as Level 2, indicating substantial improvement is possible. Largely management driven, the profile indicates the main focus is on verbal feedback, with monthly observations and data collation and analysis focused on participation and observation rates. On the other hand the second profile indicates a Level 4 process that offers improvement opportunities in ownership, training, data use, marketing and sustainability reviews. Thus the maturity ladder is a useful review tool to highlight precisely where opportunity presently exists.

Behavioral Safety Maturity Level	Ownership	Sampling Tools	Training	Observation Approach	Contact Rate	Quality of Observation	Feedback	Data Use	Sustainability Reviews	Marketing
5										
4										
3										
2										
1										

Behavioral Safety Maturity Level	Ownership	Sampling Tools	Training	Observation Approach	Contact Rate	Quality of Observation	Feedback	Data Use	Sustainability Reviews	Marketing
5										
4										
3										
2										
1										

Exhibit 2.3: Example Behavioral Safety Maturity Profiles

The five levels of the Maturity Ladder reflect many of the lessons learned from thousands of implementations on how to make Behavioral Safety successful. Whether you're just beginning or already have a process in operation, the ladder can be used as a guide to 'aim for the stars' from the start, or can help to identify areas of opportunity to improve.

The lessons learned over the years that form the base of the Maturity Ladder fall into two broad camps: Execution Issues and Technical Design. Execution refers to the strategy and components to be included in a particular process (e.g. observation focus, project team composition, outcome metrics, etc). Design refers to the technical requirements of checklist development and feedback metrics.

The knowledge base comes from multiple data sources: User surveys, academic reviews of published studies, and the authors 20 years of practical implementation and empirical experience. By and large, the results from each source accord with each other. Familiarity with the issues should help you to clear the runway for takeoff and avoid turbulence once in flight.

Using the combined CLEAR and IDEAL frameworks, the remainder of the chapter presents these Behavioral Safety lessons.

	CLEAR	IDEAL
1	Clarify the objectives	
2	Locate the problems	
3	Execute the change strategy	Identify safety related behaviors
		Develop appropriate observation checklists
		Educate everyone
		Assess ongoing safety behavior
		Limitless feedback
4	Assess current progress	
5	Review and adapt the process.	

Exhibit 2.4: Behavioral Safety Implementation Framework

Clarify the Objectives

Define Success. It is a good idea at the beginning stages to be very clear about what the process is trying to achieve and define what is meant by success. For example, reducing incidents by a minimum of 40 percent in year one is a specific, challenging but doable, and traceable success factor. Defining what is meant by success helps to focus people's attentions and actions on goal-achievement.

Match the design of the process to meet your objectives. Over the years it has become evident *'One size does not fit all'.* Your process must be flexible and robust enough to deliver outstanding results in all sorts of circumstances (e.g. dynamic working environments, lone worker situations) while retaining its integrity. The Behavioral Safety objectives *are* going to influence the process design (It is taken for granted the main objective is to reduce incident rates). As such, it is important to match the type of Behavioral Safety process to meet them. For example, involving all employees in the safety effort may be important. If so, adopting a safety partnership or employee-led model would be appropriate. Alternatively, simply demonstrating management commitment to safety may be the goal. In this case a 'safety leadership' coaching approach may be more suitable.

In many cases, it is common for contractor companies to use Behavioral Safety at the urging of customers. The objective then becomes obtaining 'competitive advantage' and demonstrating the contractor's process is complementary to the customers own. In this case, the design will be influenced by the customer's existing process, although it is always a good idea to go beyond their expectations. Talking to them and asking about their process should at least provide information about their minimum requirements.

Contractors with an existing Behavioral Safety process could conduct gap-analyses and compare the two. The objective then becomes either enhancing their own process or adding value to the customers. In either event, it furthers 'competitive advantage'. Those whose process maturity could be assessed as 'Excelling' would certainly have clear competitive advantage over other processes rated at Levels 1-4.

Locate the Problems

Understand your cultural roadblocks. Do not under-estimate the importance of cultural issues. Conduct a 'Cultural Assessment' (see chapter 6) to identify problems and build support for the execution plan. Using multiple data collection sources (e.g. Surveys, Focus Group Exercises, Site Observations, etc.) a consistent and comprehensive picture of the most important issues affecting safety and their underlying causes is constructed. The process can then be designed to target the salient issues. These could (and should) include behavioral, system, and technical solutions (see chapter 4). Addressing all of these will lead to a much bigger impact and make it easier to execute the Behavioral Safety process, as this will help convince everyone that it is a genuine drive to improve safety performance.

In large-scale implementations (See chapter 10), the assessment results have sometimes driven completely different process designs, adapted to suit the varying objectives and issues across a multitude of locations. Assessment results have also been used for internal benchmarking purposes to provide the Corporate Safety Group with a picture of the current safety culture in each of their facilities. The message therefore, is 'never pull the shutters down when opportunities present themselves'.

Executing the Change Strategy

Historically, there have been three broad approaches to Behavioral Safety: Supervisory-led (Levels 1-2), Employee-led (Levels 3-4) and the Safety Partnership (Level 5).

Primarily implemented throughout the 1980's and early 1990's, supervisory-led processes were top-down driven processes attempting to demonstrate 'safety leadership'. Supervisors observed worker's behavior (perhaps using observation cards), and gave positive or negative feedback to employees. Some would provide positive reinforcement in the form of praise, supported by weekly celebration ceremonies where pizzas, jelly donuts and sodas were given at crew meetings. Apparent behavior change did not last once these stopped. Simple and cheap to implement, this approach did have some positive effects, but also attracted criticisms that have since been hard to dispel.

Perhaps as a reaction to these criticisms, employee-led processes evolved during the early-eighties. Still commonplace, these entail employees developing the overall process to suit their needs, conducting peer-to-peer observations and providing feedback of one type or another. In some facilities the results have been excellent. However, the downside was (and is) managerial levels often (but not always) excluded themselves from the process, leading to the common perception that Behavioral Safety processes are focused solely on employee behavior.

In the mid-nineties to the present, this led to the safety partnership approach between managers and employees. This includes employees monitoring the behavior of everyone (including managers), while managers also conduct observations, and monitor their own safety related leadership behaviors (e.g. whether or not they reviewed and closed out any corrective actions). Regular feedback is provided to all levels with some also using tangible reinforcers or incentives.

What each approach has in common is measurement and feedback. The primary differences reside in the execution and measurement strategy and the levels of managerial support. This further illustrates that Behavioral Safety comes in many guises, some more effective than others.

Develop the Execution Strategy before starting. Before introducing any change process, it has to be placed in context. Doing so will raise a number of critical issues that must be carefully considered to maximize the chances of success. At a minimum these include deciding on the [a] measurement strategy; [b] contact rate; [c] supportive infrastructure; and [d] resource requirements.

Measurement Strategy

The measurement strategy will influence incident reduction. There are four basic measurement strategies applicable to employees and managers alike: [1] one-on-one, peer-to-peer observations; [2] workgroup observations; [3] self-observations; and [4] monitoring physical outcomes. A survey of 1404 users worldwide reveals 'one-on-one' approaches are most popular (50%), followed by workgroup observations (27%), self-observations (13%), and outcomes (10%).

One-on-one approaches refer to an individual monitoring another individual for a few minutes, and giving verbal feedback. This approach requires as many people as possible to become observers, and people willing to be observed. As such, it can take a great deal of time and effort to recruit and train sufficient people and to sustain their motivation over the longer term.

Workgroup observation approaches refer to one of the workgroup members, monitoring the behavior of all their colleagues during a single 10-15 minute observation. Group members rotate into the observer role every few months when checklists are updated. In this way, every workgroup member eventually becomes an observer focused on relevant safety behaviors.

Self-observations refer to people monitoring their own safety behavior and providing their own feedback. Often this approach is used with lone-workers (e.g. drivers) or where there are extreme levels of distrust between managers and employees.

Outcomes refer to the observation of the results of someone's behavior (e.g. chain hooks left hanging in walkways). In essence this approach is focused more on unsafe conditions than behaviors, but is very useful in plants (e.g. petrochemicals) where there are few people actually working.

In terms of average incident reduction, a workgroup approach is most effective, followed by a focus on 'outcomes', and 'one-on-one' approaches. Little hard evidence is available for determining the impact of self-observations, but case studies and personal experience suggest it can be effective. Thus, *popularity is not an indicator of effectiveness*. In static settings (e.g. manufacturing) the evidence suggests a 'workgroup' approach reduces incidents *10 times more* than a 'one-on-one' approach. A focus on 'outcomes' also reduces incidents twice as much as 'one-on-one' approaches. Conversely, 'outcome' and 'one-on-one' approaches are 4-5 times more effective on average, than 'workgroup' approaches in dynamic settings (e.g. construction).

It makes sense, therefore, to *consider the type of setting your process is designed for*. Of course, it may prove useful to use more than one approach to suit your circumstances. For example, in a manufacturing facility, a workgroup process would make sense with people permanently working on a particular line or in an office. A one-on-one approach may work best with facility maintenance crews when they are out on the plant. Equally, sales people driving to and from a client's premises or managers attending business meetings may find a self-observation approach more appropriate. In some companies, all their fatalities are related to moving traffic incidents: a self-observation approach could be very useful to overcome this.

Contact Rates

The frequency of data sampling will determine the degree of incident reduction. Contact rate refers to the frequency of data collection, without which continual improvement just could not happen. There are three contact rate schedules commonly used in Behavioral Safety: [1] daily; [2] intermittently (2-4 times per week); and [3] weekly. In some applications, the contact rate is as low as one observation, per person, per month or quarter. The survey of 1404 users revealed a weekly contact rate is the most popular (47%), followed by daily (41%) and intermittent contact (12%). In terms of incident reduction, the review study shows daily contact is 6.5 times more effective than a weekly contact rate. Intermittent contact is 5 times more effective than weekly.

This illustrates that higher contact rates lead to greater injury reductions. The financial benefits (Return on Investment) will far outweigh any perceived 'lost-opportunity' costs.

Supportive Infrastructure

Ineffective support will be a 'deal breaker'. It's imperative to ensure there is an effective support infrastructure for the process. This will include project teams, managerial support, management systems, communications, and marketing efforts, as well as financial and corrective action resources.

Project Teams

The willingness of people to become and stay involved in the process rests almost entirely on the performance of those driving the project. Major upsets have been experienced from poorly motivated and/or performing project teams. Equally, excellent results have been obtained from a handful of dedicated and committed people. Important considerations, therefore, surround the composition of the project team, management involvement and organizational system support. In essence, a supportive infrastructure refers to the many people involved in developing, introducing, maintaining and sustaining the process. These should include the project design team, managers, the different work area employees, the trades unions, the sites safety committee, and the safety group (e.g. advisors and managers).

Project teams refer to those who will develop, drive and support the data collection and corrective action process. There are two common formats: [1] a dedicated full-time project team, comprising of a champion (usually a senior manager), a project coordinator (usually a supervisor or employee) and an administration clerk; or [2] a site steering committee. This committee is usually comprised of 5-12 part-time individuals drawn from across the facility who meet on a monthly (or more frequent basis) to drive project execution. It is recommended that 70 percent of these are front-line employees. Each member plays a different role, ranging from project 'ambassador' to data entry clerk.

The most popular option appears to be the use of steering committees (65%), followed by a single full-time coordinator (16%), and a 2-4-man project team (10%). Some use safety personnel (8%) to drive everything. The advantages of a dedicated project team is that the speed of implementation is much more rapid, with decision-making being almost instantaneous, and appropriate corrective actions being made in real time. The advantages of a steering committee are site-wide representation and distribution of the workload. The disadvantages of a small project team relate to sickness absenteeism and vacation periods: Alternative cover has to be provided. The disadvantage of most steering committees is their part-time nature: Everything takes so much longer to implement and responsibility for action can become diffused. As such it is important to clarify each member's role (see chapter 5).

Of course, it is possible to integrate both team formats. For example, have a small, dedicated project team who drive and maintain the project on a daily basis. In addition, create a steering committee drawn from representatives from each shift or location who meet for an hour or more once per month to pass on feedback about progress, adaptations or innovations to each other and the project team.

Managerial Support

Management's commitment and leadership is one of the most important elements of the process. Research shows it can exert a 35 to 51 percent impact on employee safety behavior, providing hard evidence for the necessity of good safety leadership.

The degree of involvement has differed, however, across processes. For example, most (47%) have between 1 and 10 managers actively involved as Champions. These are people who act as mentors to help their colleagues master all aspects of the process and facilitate corrective actions. Others include many more managers (22%) while some do not have any (31%). Those processes not supported by managers may work for a while, but they will limp along and ultimately spiral into failure.

Management Systems

Begin integrating the process into the mainstream safety management system from the outset. One of the keys to a successful process is to ensure it does not become just another 'flavor of the month' initiative or 'add-on' program. Once this 'label' becomes attached, the perception is the process is only going to be short-lived. This then becomes a self-fulfilling prophecy, and it dies out after a relatively short time.

Integration takes some thought and effort, but readily available mechanisms include [a] using Risk Assessments and/or Job Safety Analyses (JSA) to help drive the development and/or adaptation of checklists; [b] using the data collected to highlight opportunities for improvement in both Managerial and Technical Systems, JSA's, Risk Assessments and Standard Operating Procedures; [c] linking peoples Behavioral Safety training to their Personnel Records and Performance Appraisals; [d] using the technologies employed to improve Ergonomics, Incident Investigations, Quality, Environmental, Health, and Production issues, etc. In turn the effect will be to assist in the long-term sustainability and adaptation of the Behavioral Safety process. Both SABIC UK and Milliken & Company, in South Carolina are exemplary examples of this.

Communications / Publicity

Communicate, Communicate, and Communicate. This essentially refers to a concerted and consistent marketing effort to keep your process alive. Research has shown safety communication is directly and strongly linked to people's safety behavior, *independently* of other safety related activities. This includes safety information seeking, safety communication expectations and people's satisfaction with safety communications. As such, it is very, very important to communicate information about the Behavioral Safety process (and safety in general), whenever and wherever you can. This includes its purpose, its progress and its impact. Surprisingly, only 39 percent of users consider this an important aspect of their process.

Limits exist only in your mind. Think hard about how to effectively communicate the need for the process, how to sell it to all, how to provide information about ongoing progress, and how to involve people (after all communication *is* a two-way process). Keep in mind *'a communication not received is not a communication at all'.*

Practical communication methods include [a] the development of a site or company-wide Behavioral Safety newsletter; [b] 'face to face' presentations from process champions, coordinators, steering committee members and frontline staff; [c] integration into safety orientations for new hires / contractors and visitors; [d] worker designed safety slogans, logos and posters; [e] small group discussions about ways to improve the process; [f] feedback about results (see below); [g] a Behavioral Safety conference or safety day, etc. Centering these on a 'branded' and polished publicity campaign has proven most effective (see chapter 9).

Resource Allocation

Under resourced Behavioral Safety processes fail. Resources fall into two categories: People and Things.

In terms of 'People', the largest resource is time. Regardless of the process design, this includes project team members, observers (data collectors), supportive managers and workforce involvement. People will need training and time to undertake the necessary actions associated with their role.

In terms of 'Things', the project team driving the process will require office space containing all the necessary equipment (e.g. telephones, computers, photocopiers, etc.). Budgets or access to the appropriate systems to facilitate any corrective actions arising from the observations or analysis of the data is also very important. Budgets may also need to be allocated for the purchasing of celebratory items to promote the process or publicize successes.

Identifying Safety Related Behaviors

Analyze your incidents for injury triggering behaviors to focus your efforts. Many skip this step when developing their process and develop a scattergun approach. They ask people to look for anything they feel is unsafe and record it (similar to near-miss reporting). Others skip this step, because they have 'borrowed' an existing observation card from somewhere else, and feel there is no need. In both cases, the process is less likely to impact the incident rate, simply because it is not targeting the real issues.

Incident databases are data libraries full of hidden treasures. But like any library, specific information resides in specific locations and can be hard to locate. The trick is to have some kind of structure (i.e. filing index) and know what you are looking for.

Most companies record and assign lost-time, minor and near-hit incidents into source categories. Some will use the classic safety structure (e.g. struck by, exposure to, contact with, striking against, etc.), while others will develop and use their own (e.g. ergonomics, materials handling, tools and equipment, etc). These should be analyzed to identify locations linked to high incident rates, the type of injury occurrences, and the tasks being done at the time of the incident. Data-mining techniques should be used to uncover hidden patterns so that future behavior can be predicted, although a simple frequency count will highlight the areas that warrant further attention. At the very least, opportunities for change to the existing database are presented if it does not lend itself to these analyses.

Develop Appropriate Observation Checklists

The design of observation sampling tools affects the quality of data collection and impact on incident rates. There is an infinite variety of sampling tools commonly used in Behavioral Safety, that fall into two broad categories: Cards and Checklists.

Cards can be 'blanks' with no predefined categories or behaviors. Blank cards *'on their own'*, are not very useful as they do not focus on the 20 percent or so of repeat behaviors responsible for the lion's share of the incidents. It is a 'scattergun' approach that tries to fix everything all at once, without any real focus. They are also based on the notion that everyone knows what an unsafe behavior is, which is not necessarily the case. In fact, people often simply report unsafe conditions.

Some cards come with a set of pre-determined categories (e.g. PPE), which contain sets of general 'catch-all' behaviors (e.g. Head, Arms & Hands, Trunk, Legs & Feet). They are often accompanied by a long list of operational definitions to guide observers when data sampling (often 4 columns spread over 2 pages). These can be useful if developed from scratch *in-house*, based on the facilities historical incident rates. Often they are not: They have been 'borrowed' from elsewhere on cost and/or speed grounds. A false economy! Processes using these types of card often take years to significantly reduce incidents related to the targeted behaviors.

Observation checklists focused on specific incident causing behaviors lead to faster and long-lasting incident reduction. A clear goal is the centerpiece of Six Sigma and other quality improvement efforts. Goal-setting research shows us that the more specific a goal is, the bigger the impact. Each specific behavior on a checklist is an explicit target (i.e. a goal) that is directing people's attentions and actions to control it. Because of its clarity, people have no doubts about what comprises the safe behavior. Specific goals also motive people to try harder and persevere more, than vague or do-your-best goals that can be interpreted in a number of ways. Processes using checklists focused on very specific behaviors tend to reduce the incident rate much more rapidly than others.

Educate Everyone

Obtain 'buy-in' before starting. The purpose of obtaining 'buy-in' is to inform people about the process, how it works, what it means to them personally, and how they can support it. Too many processes do not 'brief' or educate their staff about Behavioral Safety *before they start implementation*. They often do this when they are ready to go 'live' 3-9 months in, by which time rumors have set many misperceptions that often lead to 'kickback' or 'apathy'. The project team's main focus is then diverted to increasing and maintaining involvement in the face of self-created obstacles, rather than resolving the underlying safety issues triggering unsafe behavior.

Train your project team. People need to have the knowledge, skill and abilities early in the process if is to become sustainable and successful. Training reduces the project team member's uncertainty about how to implement a Behavioral Safety process. In turn, their confidence becomes strong enough for them to believe problems are simply challenges looking for solutions.

Train every manager to be a safety leader. Management support is critical for success, but often managers do not know what to do and/or have little knowledge about safety. In addition to aligning all management levels with the overall process, training them to observe people's behavior and provide coaching and feedback is simple and doable. This helps to create the 'safety partnership' so vital for success. The benefits also spill over into other areas (e.g. production). BP, Chevron, ExxonMobil, Shell, and other Oil & Gas majors take great pains to ensure all managers (including the most senior executives) are active safety leaders. All managers are also held accountable for safety performance (i.e. poor safety is a career limiting step!). Over the past decade, the worldwide results show a dramatic 66 percent decrease in Oil & Gas lost-time and recordable injuries.

Train all staff in coaching and feedback skills. One-on-one, peer-to-peer processes require everyone to be trained as an observer. The rationale is 'more hands make light work'. Certainly, this approach ensures everyone understands the process and the contribution each person can make (in a sense everyone is trained to be a safety leader). Many of these processes are voluntary, i.e. you only have to observe if you want to. Others mandate that everyone observe, often accompanied by quotas. Available evidence suggests that mandated processes are more successful than voluntary processes, but the quality of observations arising from quotas can be problematic. Many processes relying on just a few volunteer observers have eventually failed.

Workgroup approaches only require the 'current' active observer to be trained, with new people rotating into the role every 4-6 months or so. Eventually, everybody becomes an observer. Many of these processes are also voluntary, but some are mandatory with people asked 'who wants to go first'.

In either event, the aim is to train everyone in the organization in observation, coaching and feedback skills.

Assess Ongoing Safety Behavior

Processes not collating and using observation data fail. The whole purpose of performance data collection is to assess ongoing change and identify underlying issues that require corrective actions. There is not much point in collecting data and ignoring it. Surprisingly, this happens with at least one-third of processes. The data is not collated or analyzed. This would be unthinkable for production and quality processes! The same should apply to safety. The data can be used in many ways. For example, trending is used to establish a 'baseline' of behavioral performance, which can be used to set improvement targets, provide feedback, or identify problematic work processes (e.g. tanker unloading) causing dips in performance. However, some form of software is required to facilitate this.

Too often, processes rely solely on verbal feedback at the point of contact. This can make people feel they are the problem not part of the solution, as the perception is created the company does not want to identify and resolve underlying issues.

Limitless Feedback

Feedback is the key to performance. Although feedback comes in many shapes and forms, it *has* to be specific, relevant, credible, frequent, timely, and linked to action sources, for it to be effective. A tall order! It is important to understand that creating any process is just mechanics, until such time as it delivers feedback. The breakfast of champions, feedback provides the essential knowledge that facilitates adjustments in performance. Research evidence shows processes using three to four of the feedback mechanisms reduced twice as many injuries than those only using one or two. The overall message, therefore, is *'to use it, is to make it useful'*.

There are four basic feedback mechanisms used in Behavioral Safety: [1] verbal feedback at the point of contact; [2] graphical progress charts; [3] tabulated data analysis; and [4] group discussions of the tabulated data. Behavioral Safety processes should use as many of these feedback mechanisms as possible to reduce injuries and benefit from potential cost savings.

Assess Current Progress

Assessing current progress maximizes value. To ensure the process is going to meets its objectives, it is important to maintain a watchful eye on progress, as this facilitates any necessary corrective adjustments in 'real-time'.

The most common indicator used in Behavioral Safety is the percent safe score. This can be analyzed by each individual behavior, category, or the overall checklists to determine which are changing in the right direction by workgroup, shift, department, etc. In my view the greater the level of detail, the more impact you can assert on safety performance. However, not all processes calculate the Percent Safe score as it depends on the type of observation sampling tool used and strategies recommended by particular advisors.

The online user survey indicated the next most common indicators are the actual number of observations completed (67%), the number of near-hits turned in (56%), and the number of corrective actions completed (45%). Safety leadership behavior, the amount of constructive feedback given, and the number of active observers are also tracked by 42%. Less common is the amount of positive praise given (34%) and the number of weekly feedback meetings (29%). I would urge readers to use all of these if possible. At the very least, track those most fundamental to the improvement of safety performance: Percent Safe, Safety Leadership, and the Corrective Action Rate. The project teams should monitor these indicators, and a summary presented to the sites senior management team on a weekly basis.

Review and Adapt the Process.

Behavioral Safety processes need constant attention. Behavioral Safety processes can fade away if left to fend for themselves. Meta-analysis of 73 Behavioral Safety implementations in the USA shows 13 fell over in the first year, 25 in the second, 19 in the third, and 11 in the fourth, with only 7 lasting for at least five years. A salutary lesson!

Just like financial, production, and quality systems, a Behavioral Safety process needs constant management attention. In-depth management reviews are necessary to obtain a 'big picture' view. These assess whether the process is meeting its goals and objectives and include an evaluation of *system* performance based on existing data (review inputs). It should also address any decisions or actions necessary to improve the process. Ideally, people divorced from its day-to-day operation to provide an impartial and detached view, conduct the reviews. In the first year or so, mini reviews will help to embed the process so it becomes a way of life, but annual reviews are essential to ensure its longevity.

Summary

Presenting a Behavioral Safety Maturity Ladder to guide your efforts, this chapter has reflected on some very real lessons learned over the past 20 years or so. These make the point that Behavioral Safety is not a magic wand that can be waved to automatically cure all ills forever and a day. It is evident that introducing and maintaining a Behavioral Safety processes should not be undertaken lightly. It will take a consistency of focus, purpose, and execution from all concerned to ensure sustainable success. Once achieved, the results can be very dramatic.

3 Should You Use Professional Assistance?

Alex, a Safety Manager of a 3000 strong manufacturing company, wanted to do something about rising incident rates, but 30 percent budgetary cutbacks meant little room for maneuver. He asked other safety professionals for advice on what to do. With good intentions, a colleague e-mailed him copies of an observation card and a user's handbook, with a note explaining that Behavioral Safety processes could be the answer to his prayers. All he had to do was change the name on the observation card, introduce it in his company and 'hey presto', incidents would disappear.

Calling it 'Safety First', he had 36,000 observation cards printed with categories that covered Personal Protective Equipment (PPE), Potential Injury Causes, Tools and Equipment, Procedures and Orderliness, Environment, and Health. He had the cards put in all the operational areas in boxes so they were readily available. Photocopied handbooks were distributed, with instructions for everyone to observe another at least once per month, fill out the cards and send them back to the safety department. He followed this up in the company newsletter with information obtained from the Internet about how safety observations would improve the company's incident rates and how it was in everybody's interests.

In the first Quarter, around 160 cards were handed in. Alex would review these at the end of each month. Ninety percent of them indicated everyone was wearing their PPE. Somewhat disappointed, but expecting some teething problems, Alex asked all the production supervisors to 'promote' the observations on their shifts. This led to 200 cards coming in, but Alex noticed they were almost always from the same few people.

In the third quarter, attempting to get more people involved, Alex offered a $250 incentive to the person who handed in the most cards in a month. Alex was flooded with cards, with over 200 of them focused on PPE from one person, but with different writing! He went to the floor to speak to the person, and found him taking a bundle of completed observation cards out of his tool bag. Red-faced, the guy explained he had got his wife and children to complete them at home so he could claim the prize! Annoyed, Alex dropped the incentive.

In the fourth quarter the number of cards dropped to a trickle. Incident rates had also stayed the same throughout the year. Disappointed at the supposed power of the Behavioral Safety approach, Alex began to search for something else that would improve the company's incident rates.

Over the past three decades, thousands of companies around the world have implemented Behavioral Safety. Primarily the uptake has been in manufacturing, oil and gas, chemicals, and construction; although a wide range of other industries have also followed suit. Many of these have become frustrated over the years, as their processes have stalled due to people's lack of interest, with these companies seeking ways to revitalize their process. Others have fallen over, never to be resuscitated. Many cannot understand what went wrong, so they turn their backs on the process and abandon it to look for the next 'miracle cure'.

Alex's 'self-help' approach clearly did not work. He adapted an existing observation process from somewhere else with great expectation, but limited knowledge. I have seen too many similar examples often driven by the need to 'do something' and to do it 'on the cheap'. To introduce an effective Behavioral Safety process requires detailed knowledge about designing a process that suits the circumstance. This also needs to include information on how to introduce, implement, maintain and sustain the process in the most cost-effective manner.

Alex certainly made some classic mistakes. The first was to 'borrow' someone else's process, without considering whether the card was targeting the real problems in his facility. The second was to simply impose it on people, and expect people to buy-in to it without really explaining what people had to do and why. The third was Alex's reliance on people reading the 'handbook' and following the instructions, instead of physically training people in observation and coaching skills. The fourth was to simply count the number of cards turned in and the names of those completing them. He should have collated the data in a useful format, provided feedback and followed through on corrective actions. The fifth was to incentivize the number of cards completed, which led to 'cheating'. The mistakes Alex made provide a strong case for professional assistance.

Knowing When Help is Needed.

It's logical to abandon a process because the costs consistently outweigh the benefits: i.e. there is no payback for the buck. However, most companies will have invested a lot of time, money and effort into the process. It makes good commercial sense, therefore, to discover what went wrong before 'throwing out the baby with the bathwater'. A good clue that some assistance is required for an existing process is when the process project teams are struggling to make the process work as intended. Alex struggled alone, but with a little help, his process could have been turned around to deliver its intended benefits.

The visible cues to a failing process are many and varied. Common cues are employee withdrawal, or reluctance to take part. In general, (assuming a reasonably good process has been introduced in the right way) the process is not delivering for them. For example, corrective actions are not being pursued, the observation data is being faked (and everyone knows it), management are disinterested, no one attends meetings because of time squeezes, the guys weren't involved in its development, etc.

There are many people with the right expertise to assist in either adapting your process, or helping you start. The trick for both routes is finding the right person or company (see below). If you simply want help adapting your existing process to meet your needs, you should invite your chosen advisor to examine the process for a day or two. They will look at the performance measures, talk to people about the process to discover their likes and dislikes, and what the problems and preferred solutions are. This should conclude in a written report giving strategic direction and tactical advice from an objective and experienced viewpoint to help get your process back on track.

Information Seeking

If you are starting from scratch, you need solid information to make informed decisions.

Limited knowledge about how to develop, run and maintain a Behavioral Safety process is obviously a drawback, as Alex showed. Anyone thinking of doing so, should research the implications before starting. The information is everywhere. Sister companies, industry and professional associations, the Internet, and consultancies are just a few readily available examples.

Many 'user' companies are justifiability proud of their process. They are keen to show visitors what they have achieved and are willing to discuss the challenges they faced, the help they got, and where it came from. Industry and professional associations will also often have a view, contained in documentation posted on their websites. Many companies also post PowerPoint presentations and other information on the Internet, about the success or otherwise of their process. This material is worth viewing. It will give you good inside information to assist your determinations about whether or not you need professional assistance.

Consultant companies will also provide you with basic information if you call them. Remember, though, that even genuine experts will agree on many things, but differ on others (that's why they are experts - they have studied the field and understand the subtle differences). The information you receive from professional advisors should be compared to the knowledge you have gained from other sources. This will also help satisfy you they are genuine experts.

Helping Yourself

Before deciding on professional assistance you should examine your needs and aim to *avoid seeking help on matters that you should be handling yourself.* For example, you should sell the idea of doing Behavioral Safety to your management team. If you have taken the time and trouble to seek out the appropriate information, you should have obtained their backing and authorization prior to seeking assistance. This will require you to present them with the facts that you have obtained from your research. This also helps them separate the 'wheat from the chaff' when professionals 'arrive on their doorstep' to discuss approach, strategy and pricing.

Other things you should do include examining your incident database for patterns of incidents that cannot be readily explained. The purpose is to know why Behavioral Safety is going to be helpful. Give thought to the technological or management system issues involved in these incidents. In other words, how confident are you that most of your problems arise from people's behavior.

If you are certain the triggers and causes are behavioral in nature, explore whether or not you have the necessary knowledge, competence and skills 'in-house'. A worldwide user survey showed 14% of companies had 'in-house' experience in the Corporate Safety

Department. Others (24%) employed people with previous experience, while some (5%) directly copied the processes of companies they visited. However, there is no direct evidence to indicate if these were success of failures. Thus, even with 'in-house' experience, professional assistance should still be considered.

If satisfied that professional assistance is appropriate, scope out precisely [1] the problem as you see it; [2] why an 'in-house' solution is not realistic; [3] what you want the professional advisor to do; and [4] what will count as a successful outcome.

Provide a written brief to bring potential advisors 'up to speed'. The brief should contain [1] background information about the company and its activities; [2] how many people will be involved; [3] a clear statement about the Behavioral Safety objectives; [4] success criteria; [5] a precise description of the problem; [6] potential time frames; and [7] a summary of the company's recent injury history. The more potential advisors know about the issues, the more they will be able to help you.

Choosing a Partner
As in any field there are many offering professional 'Behavioral Safety' assistance. These firms come in all shapes and sizes, with varying degrees of experience and track records. It can be difficult separating those with genuine expertise from those with a less impressive background. As many as 36 companies from around the world recently attended a pre-tender meeting with a large company to implement Behavioral Safety in all their facilities. Of those, only 6 were considered genuine contenders with a demonstrable track record obtained over the last decade or two. The rest were 'wannabes' with little or no experience. In this particular case, the ratio between knowledgeable companies and 'wannabes' was 1 in 6.

A quick 'Google' shows there are literally hundreds of safety and risk management consultancies who offer a Behavioral Safety service in amongst all their other safety products (I've even seen ex-special forces security consultancies offering Behavioral Safety!). As far as some are concerned anything to do with behavior and safety must, by definition, be 'Behavioral Safety'. A few websites even offer to sell 'templates' of checklists, Behavioral Safety manuals, etc, without offering any 'back-up' service at all! Some offering these 'tools' *are* experts in safety / risk management, but that does not make them experts in Behavioral Safety.

Nobody would willingly choose a general medical practitioner to conduct open-heart surgery on him or her. But, companies often choose professional assistance from someone with expertise in a related field who gives wrong advice because they do not understand the intricacies. As Deming famously once said *'Does experience help? NO! Not if we are doing the wrong things'*. Too often, Behavioral Safety processes fail because companies *have* been advised to do the wrong things. In my experience, Behavioral Safety is often a 'one time deal': If you get it wrong, frontline employees will not want anything to do with it again for a very long time, if at all.

True Expertise

Genuine 'Behavioral Safety' expertise is evident by a combination of factors. First, Behavioral Safety is the person or company's core activity: It is the mainstay of their livelihood. In other words, their *'Raison d'être'* is centered on knowing about and applying Behavioral Safety in all its glory. Second, they have a long and strong implementation history across a multitude of industries. This means they know when certain strategies and particular designs are appropriate and know where to look to navigate the 'tripwires'. Third, they have a consistent, documented track record of injury reduction. *We are what we repeatedly do. Excellence, therefore, is not an act but a habit.* Fourth, the company is widely recognized for contributing to the development of Behavioral Safety knowledge. Contributions to the advancement of a discipline require 'in-depth' knowledge and practical experience. These also demonstrate the advisor is on a 'continual improvement' journey. Finally, they are willing to 'put their money where their mouth is'. Most experts are willing to guarantee their process will deliver reductions in incident rates *provided their advice is followed.*

Genuine expertise, therefore, comes from living and breathing the subject matter, applying it in the real world for an extensive period of time, consistently proving the process delivers quantifiable benefits, continually looking to improve and add value, and having sufficient confidence to guarantee results.

Background Qualifications

There are no 'formal' qualifications to become a Behavioral Safety advisor. In practice, three disciplines produce the vast majority of Behavioral Safety advisors: Psychology, Safety, and Management.

Many advisors have a background in psychology and hold PhD's. However, PhD psychologists are not automatic Behavioral Safety experts! According to Wikipedia there are some 68 sub-disciplines of psychology. The most relevant for Behavioral Safety would be Applied Behavioral Analysts and Industrial / Organizational (I/O) psychologists. People from these two backgrounds possess a fundamental understanding of Behavioral Theory and its application. I/O psychologists, by definition, also possess a deeper understanding of the many processes at play in the world of work. However, safety is not usually a part of the education of either psychology sub-disciplines (although I/O psychologists do touch on the basics of ergonomics and human factors).

Many advisors have previously held positions as safety professionals. Some hold higher degrees in safety management and have achieved professional status via additional experience and examination. By definition, they are experts in safety management, but are not necessarily a 'Behavioral Safety' expert. Relatively few have been heavily involved in Behavioral Safety processes. Of these, many have often taken a detached managerial overview of a process, rather than driven and implemented themselves. Without doubt this has given them insights into what works and what does not, but it does not necessarily qualify them to advise others on the subject.

Many others have either been through business school and/or employed in management functions and have in-depth understanding of management processes, organizational behavior and business practices. Some of their experience would be relevant (e.g. Six Sigma), but it is not sufficient in and of itself, for the person to be deemed a Behavioral Safety advisor.

A few advisors are ex-tradesmen with extensive experience of implementing an 'in-house' or consultant firm's Behavioral Safety process. These guys have worked their way up through the safety or management functions. Without doubt, they possess a deep understanding of the details involved in a particular process, the way the 'workforce' thinks & acts, and management systems. The vast majority, however, do not possess full knowledge or understanding of the relevant underpinning theories.

On the basis of this brief tour, the ideal Behavioral Safety advisor would obviously be an ex-tradesperson, possess appropriate academic qualifications and have gained professional experience in all three disciplines. A very rare breed! In reality, people with a mix of academic knowledge from one or more of these disciplines, coupled with real-world experience of the others, and an extensive background in learning and applying Behavioral Safety processes across a range of industries would represent the ideal.

Experience

It is clear that professional advisors qualifications are not necessarily the sole basis for decision-making, though they do allow you to establish their credibility. Experience of Behavioral Safety implementations would be the next biggest factor to assess. This divides into the experience of the professional advising firm and their individual advisors: the two are not always the same due to staff turnover.

Pertinent questions to ask of firms revolve around their length of time implementing Behavioral Safety in industry, their approach, how their process has changed over time to add value, the experience of their individual advisors, and their track record of substantially impacting incident rates. For example, asking how one advisors approach differs from others would allow you to compare which was most likely to meet your objectives. You may also follow up with probing their experience in your particular industry. A note of caution however, the principles of Behavioral Safety are universally applicable. They can be applied to safety issues in any industry, even if the advisor has never operated in that one previously.

Even so, every industry believes its safety issues are uniquely different from others, as do companies within a particular sector. At one level this is true: Aviation, Mining, Oil & Gas exploration for example are faced with unique challenges arising from their *modus operandi*. The safety issues in most, however, are all of a likeness. For example, the behavior of not wearing PPE is going to be the same across all industries: it is just the type that differs for different tasks. In my first Patient Safety implementation, we significantly reduced the Hospital Acquired Infection (HAI) rate by 70 percent in just six months. Other advisors have achieved similar outcomes during their first foray into a particular industry (e.g. Electricity distribution, Logging, Oil & Gas, etc.).

Questions to ask about individual advisors (mostly employed by the firms) relate to their years of direct 'hands-on' experience, with more obviously adding more weight. Many tender documents specify junior team members must possess an average of five years experience and ten years for senior team members. This seems perfectly reasonable, given the amount of time, effort and money the company will expend introducing and maintaining the process. However, many companies also recognize the need to bring on 'apprentices', and allow some junior team members with less than five years to participate under the close guidance of highly experienced senior project managers. Ideally, every advisor is able to relate to, and communicate with everyone in a company: from the CEO to the janitor.

Approach

Even among the world's top five professional Behavioral Safety advisors there is a diversity of approach. Some are based almost entirely on Behavioral Technology, while others are a mix of Behavioral Technology, Psychology, General Management Theory, and Safety Management. In other words, approaches range from a sole focus on the psychology of safety, to those with an emphasis on improving a company's entire safety culture. For example, some will focus almost entirely on identifying and reinforcing the behaviors of individuals. Others are more 'management system' orientated underpinned by continual improvement cycles. Though each approach has validity, each reflects the learning history or 'theoretical roots' of the 'advisor' and often dictates their process design and application.

Some offer pre-packaged solutions that can be bought 'off the shelf' comprising training, documentation and videos, while others offer more flexible, customized processes to ensure 'best-fit'. A rule of thumb is that smaller professional companies offer more flexible solutions, while larger companies offer 'standardized' pre-packaged solutions. Regardless, be very wary if the process offered is not specifically designed to meet your process and outcome success criteria. This is why it is so important for you to do your homework and research the approach that is best suited for your needs and circumstances. It is vital to ensure the chosen process is structured, flexible and adaptable to your specific needs, perhaps across multiple locations.

Ideally, the advisors process should be able to [1] identify frequent injury causing behaviors and their links to associated managerial and technical systems; [2] fully involve both management and employees within the same process (not as separate add-ons); [3] include data collection, collation and analysis; [4] provide feedback to appropriate levels; and [5] be integrated with other management systems and improvement strategies to complement wider company goals (See chapter 5). In addition, a good process will have clear implementation milestones and defined 'value-adding' success 'outcomes' attached to each part of the process.

Narrow Down the Field

Armed with the 'in-depth' analysis of your issues and objectives, identify potential professional advisors. If you have visited other companies as part of your initial research, the name of their professional advisor would be known. If not, the Internet is a good place to start. Most authentic advisors have websites, many of whom display their client's names and case histories. If possible, call these clients and ask them about their experiences with the process and the professional firm. Of course, attending Behavioral Safety conferences is also a good place to meet those already implementing Behavioral Safety, those thinking about it and, more often than not, genuine professional advisors. These activities should help narrow down the list of potential advisors to a manageable number. When conducting reference checks ask about both implementation and the amount of follow up support received and its nature.

Goodness of Fit

Request the chosen pool of professional advisors to either submit a written proposal and/or present to a joint management - employee selection team. There are three basic assessment criteria: Expertise,

Fit and Price. At this stage, the expertise of the selected candidate pool should already be known. You are primarily examining the advisors potential fit with your company and whether you will receive value for money.

Fit covers three issues: People, Schedule and Scope. In terms of 'People fit', assess their likeability, professionalism and whether they are appropriate for your people & culture. They could be working inside your company for a long time. This is a critical issue, as whilst they might be able to do the work, if they can't work harmoniously with your people the results will be less than optimal. In terms of 'Schedule fit' ensure the proposed schedule of works matches the timeframe you have set to meet your objectives. If the objectives are not met within the appropriate time-scale, company people's credibility and reputation could be at stake. In terms of 'Scope fit', do the proposed process and its individual elements comply with *all* your requirements and needs?

'Fit analyses' allow you to determine how the advisor relates to people, how knowledgeable they are, how professional they are, and whether there is a good 'match' for a potential long-term partnership. You should probe them about their approach to ensure it is going to help meet your objectives, and over what time frame (some take twice as long as others to implement).

Price

Pricing can be a contentious issue: The client wants the best possible service, with tangible results, for the lowest prices possible. The advisor wants to provide the best possible service, achieve tangible results, and ensure a realistic return on his or her investment. The best way to satisfy both parties is to ensure the advisor will add-value to your company, and in return be rewarded appropriately: A win-win for all concerned.

There are three basic pricing models: Value-based; Hourly rate and Fixed price. Usually, travel, accommodation and subsistence expenses are also added to professional advisors quotations.

Value-based refers to the advisor fees being based on a sliding scale, based on results achieved. The goal is to align price with the value delivered. If the advisor exceeds expectations, they are paid more. If the advisor fails to meet expectations they are paid less. In this way, both parties are heavily invested in the success of the process. In a nutshell, the project's dollar value to the company is established and the advisor charges a portion of that value.

Hourly rate refers to billing for the estimated man-hours to be spent on the project for the benefit of the services. A standard measuring stick, the hourly rate gives a company an apples-to-apples price comparison of their alternatives. However, the company is actually buying effort not necessarily success (the two are often confused due to the high expectations of results).

Fixed price refers to a flat-fee for all works done, inclusive of materials, manpower, etc and payment does not depend on the amount of resources or time expended. This puts the project risks onto the advisor, but helps to control company costs. However, no plan is foolproof and no one can be completely prepared for the future. If the advisor's costs exceed the fixed price, cost over-runs become likely. If the company does not renegotiate, the advisor may simply walk away.

Deming reminds us price has no meaning without a measure of the quality being purchased. If low pricing guarantees low quality anywhere in the process, then the final product, though it may be cheap, will also be of low quality. Paying a premium for genuine expertise will cost more than less adept advisors, but 'low quality' could ultimately cost even more from a failed process.

Each pricing model can also affect the motivation of the advisor. The value-added model significantly increases the likelihood of success. The hourly rate increases the likelihood of contract variations if all does not go smoothly, and the number of days has been underestimated or the work scope changes due to delays within the company. The fixed price model is notorious for cost overruns and cancelled projects.

Final Preparations

Once the advisor is selected, some key issues should be addressed. First clarify the contractual details and issue the appropriate contract or purchase order. Second, clarify the start date and ensure both you and the advisor have all the logistical arrangements in place. This would include the advisor assigning the appropriate advisors to the project, and those arriving on time, with all strategies and materials prepared. Companies should have pre-arranged liaison personnel, workspaces, training rooms, and appropriate personnel ready to begin.

Summary

The overall message is *Caveat Emptor* (Let the buyer beware). Begin with a thorough analysis of your issues; define your objectives and what you mean by success. Do your homework. Investigate the process you want to meet your needs and find a small pool of suppliers with genuine expertise in addition to depth and breadth of experience. Assess them against the perceived goodness of fit with your company and its culture. Determine if the price offers value for money. Finally, choose the one you feel most comfortable with and whose work impresses you the most.

4 Underlying Principles

Mike, a manager in charge of 200 workers in a large, noisy metal fabrication factory was perplexed. He and his team had provided polymer foam earplugs but few workers wore them. Mike and his team had tried group talks, publicity campaigns and talking to individual workers. Despite this effort, he noticed most people did not wear them. Mike called a colleague and asked how they managed the issue in their factory. He was told that a behavioral approach had helped to overcome the issue. Mike contacted the consultant who had helped start their process and hired him in.

The consultant asked for historical data identifying the true extent of the problem. Because there was no hard data, the consultant talked to the workers to identify what the problems were. Most said the earplugs were uncomfortable, and they were not used to putting foreign objects in their ears, particularly as they did not think their hearing was being affected by the noise anyway. The consultant proposed two complementary solutions: [1] allow workers to trial various types of hearing protection to identify those most comfortable for them; and, [2] measure the temporary hearing loss of random workers at the beginning and end of a shift for a month. Each worker would receive individual feedback and an anonymous copy of the results would be posted for all to see. Simultaneously, earplug usage would be monitored to measure the degree of uptake during the implementation and after, for a 6 months period.

The proposal was put to Mike who readily agreed. Some members of the management team thought this was nonsense, with Jim being vehemently against it. He thought all the pussyfooting around should stop, with workers being disciplined or suspended if they did not wear them. Mike suggested Jim try it his way, while the remainder of the plant would try the behavioral approach. They would compare results, and thereafter go with the most effective method. After 6 months the results for each method were startlingly clear. Use of hearing protection increased to 90 percent in the departments using the behavioral approach. Jim's department had made no progress whatsoever. Mostly because he could not follow through with his threats of suspension, as it would have negatively impacted productivity and industrial relations.

Mike's example provides a very powerful testimony to the effectiveness of Behavioral Safety by illustrating that it works where traditional safety approaches fail. When implemented properly

Behavioral Safety uses a systematic approach based on a blend of Management, Safety, and Psychology to enhance the overall impact. For example, recognizing Behavioral Safety is an intensive, long-term effort to transform safety performance, the CLEAR process mirrors the Quality Management Planning, Organizing, Controlling, Monitoring, and Revising control loop.

Exhibit 4.1: CLEAR Process Control Loop

Clarify the Objectives

Akin to Quality Management, clarifying the objectives or goals of the Behavioral Safety process points to very clear measurable outcomes which in turn creates a sense of purpose. Mostly the objectives will have become apparent from deteriorating incident rates or specific non-conformance (or deviations) noted from weekly managerial walk rounds surrounding established safety practices (e.g. Permit to Work Systems) or from Safety Management System (SMS) reviews.

Whatever the objective, it will take planning to achieve. Every process I have ever implemented has been different, albeit within the success framework of the Process Cycle (see Chapter 1). Each time I have had to strategize to work out how the objectives are going to be achieved. This has involved detailed planning of cost-effective solutions while also minimizing resource allocation. Planning addresses the question *'How do you eat an elephant?'* Reflecting decades of managerial goal-setting research the answer is *'One piece at a time'*.

Break up your strategy into smaller chunks of activity, so that each set builds on the previous activity. Then decide on the outcomes for each activity and how you are going to measure *process progress* and *outcome success*. It is also important to obtain agreement from all other stakeholders who may be affected by the activities. In light of the day-to-day realities in your company, ensure your strategy and each activity is achievable and realistic for the time frames set. In many companies there is nothing worse than setting action targets and missing them. This can cast doubt on your credibility and that of the entire Behavioral Safety process.

Locate the Problems

Once the objectives, strategy, and the associated activities and outcomes have been set, *the real problems must be identified.* Most Behavioral Safety processes will use historical incident data as a starting point (if it is available). In the case study, hard factual data was unavailable, so other means (talking to workers) were used to discover what the problems were (a simple but powerful method). This showed [1] workers found the earplugs uncomfortable; [2] they did not like putting foreign objects in their ears; and [3] the workers did not relate their noisy environment to immediate hearing loss.

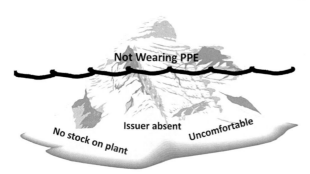

Exhibit 4.2: Iceberg View of a Presenting Problem

Thus, enquiry revealed the problem presented (non usage) was a symptom of other underlying issues (discomfort and lack of knowledge of the immediate effects). If agreeable solutions could be found, in all likelihood the objective of hearing protection usage by all would be achieved. Therefore, think of every presenting problem as the tip of an iceberg: the bit you can see. Underneath there are a host of other hidden issues!

Which Lens?

There are a number of practical discovery methods commonly used (See chapter 6) to identify the hidden issues. Many behavioral practitioners use Applied Behavioral Analysis, a systematic discovery process derived from behavioral psychology. Focused on individual behaviors this method isolates the behavior of interest, identifies the drivers (antecedents) for the behavior, and the reinforcing consequences to the person to discover what is maintaining that behavior. This analysis also identifies any system or environmental 'barriers' to safe behavior.

Those with a safety background will likely interrogate their incident databases using statistical methods to identify the issues (e.g. eye injuries) presenting the most significant areas of concern. Once identified, Risk Assessment, Job Safety Analysis, or Root Cause Analysis may be used to 'home in' on the behaviors and causation factors.

Those from a more general management background are likely to use Task Analyses, Site Observations, Interviews, and Focus Group exercises to get at the underlying drivers for unsafe behavior.

Some may even use all three approaches. This illustrates there is 'more than one way to skin a cat'. The most important aspect is to use the method(s) you feel are right for you, while ensuring the accuracy of your findings. You do not want to go down dead-end routes!

Digging Deeper

It is always a good idea to look at a problem from more than one angle. Presenting problems are often a symptom of other underlying issues such as the behavior of ineffective management systems or information technology systems. By way of illustration, in one plant I consulted for, the workers were often seen not wearing Personal Protective Equipment (PPE). When approached and asked why, the response was that PPE was always unavailable. Mystified, the management team examined the entire PPE supply chain. This showed: [1] workers were not allowed to go to the stores and request the PPE themselves. They had to ask supervisors; [2] no 'back-up' PPE stock was kept in the control rooms on the plant, so gloves, goggles, hard hats and hearing protection were not immediately available for distribution; [3] the person responsible for issuing PPE was often sick, and never arranged alternative cover; [4] the store's software system was incapable of delivering an overview of the entire PPE stock levels at the press of a few buttons. It would take at least a week, because everything was entered and queried on a type, manufacturer and size 'line-by-line' basis; and, [5] the IT department, upon instruction from the purchasing department, set the stock re-order levels. So a whole set of issues, most of which were quality related, were responsible for people not wearing PPE. This highlights that people's safety behavior is often dependent upon the effectiveness of both safety and non-safety systems.

Digging deeper also emphasizes one of the major principles of a good behavioral approach: *Identify the exact problems before venturing solutions*. This is what happened in the example case study. The advisors proposed solutions were based on more detailed information than had been obtained by site management. They obtained and used data. One solution involved trialing various types of hearing protection so that workers who wore them would feel more comfortable. Clients who have tried this have often obtained significant cost savings over the course of a year. The reason is that more comfortable PPE is actually used and not discarded all over the site (creating attendant housekeeping problems). This means purchasing & supply do not have to continuously procure more of the same uncomfortable PPE that will also be discarded.

Spin-Offs

On a more fundamental level, allowing workers to find the most comfortable PPE available meant management had not negotiated away the absolute requirement of wearing hearing protection. Rather they had negotiated the means to achieve the requirement. Representing a 'win-win', this is a good example of the 'safety partnership' in action, which respects people as individuals and involves them in safety decision-making. In turn, this creates ownership of, and commitment to, the proposed solution(s) that in turn improves performance.

The second solution was based on proving to workers the extent of their hearing loss over the course of just one day. Measuring the extent of loss and providing feedback gave the workers factual data that had personal meaning to them, not other people, which allowed them to make appropriate judgments and adjust their behavior.

Finding the Right Solutions

Good Behavioral Safety processes go beyond the obvious and target three interacting elements: Individual or Group Behavior; Managerial & Technical Systems, and Person Factors (e.g. Knowledge, Skills, or Abilities) in its search for solutions. The solutions required for the PPE supply chain example above illustrate this.

- *Behavioral solutions* include providing alternate cover for the PPE issuer when absent.
- *Technical solutions* include re-programming the software to provide a simple overview of PPE stock levels at any moment in time
- *Managerial System solutions* include [a] appropriate stock levels being set by the Safety Department, not IT or Procurement; and, [b] providing a 'back-up' PPE store in the control room so a small quantity of PPE is available to workers at a moment's notice.

Behavioral Safety processes use this interactive relationship to help create favorable conditions for doing jobs safely. If everything is in place (e.g. planning, materials, manpower, methods, and equipment) and working as intended, people will tend to behave safely. If any of these are missing, people will behave unsafely to overcome any problems, primarily just to get the job done.

Typically, Behavioral Safety solutions focus on [1] *situational* factors when obstacles in one form or another are preventing people from behaving safely; and [2] *person* factors when people do not know [a] what to do; [b] how to do something; or [c] when to do something. Usually, this lack of knowledge, skills and abilities are related to situational factors (e.g. poor human resource systems).

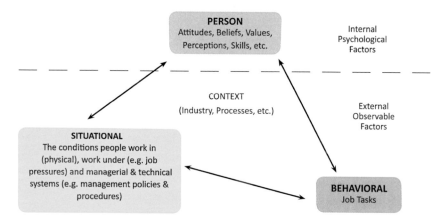

Exhibit 4.3: **Interactive Nature of Person, Situation and Behavior**

Where is the Biggest Payback?

All three elements are important, but not equally so. An emphasis on the *situation-behavior link* provides a bigger bang for the buck. Because the issues surrounding these are observable they provide the most practical means of improving safety. Corrective actions spinning out of the solutions are measurable and the results demonstrable. This is not always true for softer 'internal' person factors, though opportunities for concrete measurement do exist with knowledge, skills and ability acquisition (i.e. training).

Behavioral Safety processes *focusing solely on behavior, to the exclusion of other issues, will not bring about sustainable success.* Behavioral Safety focuses primarily on behavior because it is the common denominator underpinning safety performance, but it also recognizes that people's safety related behavior is affected by other factors that must be addressed.

Execute the Change Strategy

A useful anchor to follow for developing your change strategy is using the acronym IDEAL:

1. **I**dentify safety related behaviors
2. **D**evelop appropriate observation checklists
3. **E**ducate everyone
4. **A**ssess ongoing safety behavior
5. **L**imitless feedback

Identify Safety Related Behaviors

An important principle of a Behavioral Safety process is to *ensure it targets people's behavior at each layer of the accident causation chain*. Approximately 80-95 percent of all accidents are thought to be triggered by unsafe behaviors. Originally, these were thought to be workers behavior only. Inquiries into numerous major disasters in recent years have convinced many this is not so and managerial behaviors are now also recognized as highly significant incident causation factors.

Based on research from the US Department of Energy in the 1970's and more recent work funded by Shell, the accident causation chain consists of five layers: [1] the *Strategic* level which comprises of senior management; [2] the *Operational* level which consist of mid level line-management; [3] the *Tactical* level which refers to support function such as Human Resources, Purchasing & Supply; [4] the *Behavioral* Level, which refers primarily to employees production or service behaviors; and [5] the *Defensive* level which refers to the presence and type of control measures. The basic premise is system faults (represented as holes in Exhibit 4.4) reside, or are created by people's behavior, in each layer. On their own they are harmless, but combined with others they can breach the defenses and cause an incident. Very often, unsafe behavior is the triggering mechanism causing two or more system faults to combine.

A company that installed a new production process that involved building two new mezzanine floors in an existing plant best illustrates these principles. Plant engineers had formulated plans that had been approved by a project team over a period of time. Once the work was complete, it was found that a supporting girder had been erected at a height of five foot above the second step of a staircase on each new floor. Thus two physical faults were introduced into the physical environment during the planning and construction phases. When the new process equipment was commissioned, product blockages frequently occurred in the related pipe work. Another system fault!

Clearing the blockages required the operator to isolate the equipment at a lower production floor and climb the stairs to the top mezzanine floor to clear the pipe work. There was a sole operator responsible for two machines. If he were too slow clearing the blockage, the pipework for the other machine would also block. This meant his entire shift could be spent ascending/descending stairs to clear pipe blockages. At this point all these 'harmless' faults combined to trigger an accident when the operator ran up the stairs to clear a blockage, and ran into one of the low girders, knocking himself unconscious.

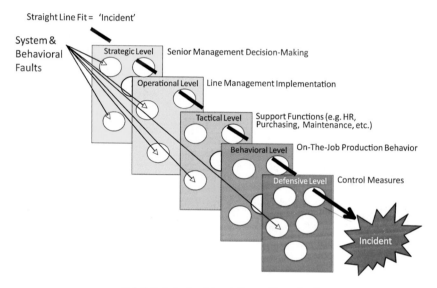

Exhibit 4.4: Accident Causation Chain

Behaviors and Levels

People's job-related behavior is the most common method for system faults to be introduced at each level, and can arise anywhere in a company, as the above illustrates. It makes sense, therefore, to help remove system faults by focusing on the safety-related job behaviors of people at each level.

At both the *'Strategic'* and *'Operational'* levels, a Behavioral Safety process could help by targeting the safety leadership behavior of the management team, to ensure safety is on their radar. At the *'Tactical'* level, the various support functions on site (e.g. Purchasing & Supply, Human Resources, Finance, Engineering, etc.) could focus on the job behaviors of those functions that directly impact the safety of production workers. At the *'Behavioral'* level the focus could be on generic sets of safety behaviors (e.g. housekeeping), specific job behaviors (e.g. tying off a ladder prior to use) or outcomes (e.g. Emergency equipment is free from obstructions). At the *'Defensive'* level the behavior of those responsible for corrective actions, management of change procedures, emergency procedures, etc., could be targeted to ensure the defensive systems are functioning as intended.

The important behaviors and situational aspects to address should come out of the problem-solving process, described previously. If they have not, perhaps because your incident rates are so low, there are a number of other sources that can be used. These include existing Risk Assessments, Job Safety Analysis, and Standard Operating Procedures, or simple site observations. More inclusive methods include Interviews or Focus Group exercises with a 'diagonal slice' of company staff (See chapter 6). It is also a good idea to ask employees about the common unsafe behaviors they see or engage in every day. If they trust you, they will tell you. If you adopt this more informal approach, ensure that you understand the reasons behind the problem behaviors. Remember, the Titanic did not see the iceberg!

Develop Appropriate Observation Checklists

Observation checklists are the hub of the measurement and data collection engine. However, checklist development is full of subtleties and requires skill (see Chapter 7). They must certainly target observable behaviors that are within people's control; and be related to the incidents in question in any given location.

Unfortunately, many companies doing Behavioral Safety skip this step. They 'borrow' a safety observation checklist from a third-party facility or purchase a Generic card from a vendor. They are often very surprised when they do not see any results!

In principle, different checklists should be developed for every department (inclusive of administration), focused on those safety-related behaviors known to be involved in incidents. Involvement of those who are going to use them and be observed against them is critical. This also holds true for the managerial safety leadership checklists targeted at each of the layers in the accident causation chain, and the job-related checklists of those in the support functions.

Educate Everyone

There are four parts to this element of the change strategy. First, the *'idea'* of the Behavioral Safety process needs to be explained to all, to obtain 'buy-in' and commitment. This should be done at the very beginning of the process. Go armed with the appropriate facts such as historical and current incident rates and trends. Explain the purpose of the process, what it is trying to achieve and how you are going to get there. Some leave this until they are on the point of 'going live'. I believe this to be a strategic mistake. The 'guys' help is needed from the very beginning if your process is going to function smoothly and become sustainable. Second, the entire management team needs to become aligned to the process. This should inform them of the likely impact of their involvement and what you require from them (See chapter 8). In essence these first two are 'Tell & Sell' information sessions. Obtaining people's commitment to the process is vital. Third, the project team or steering committee needs comprehensive training in the core principles and details of the implementation process (see chapter 5). Finally, you need to train people in observation, coaching, and feedback skills. Thus, these last two aspects are concerned with educating those people who will be heavily involved in implementation.

Assess Ongoing Safety Behavior

Assessing ongoing behavior relates to two distinct aspects. First, who is being assessed? The options include individuals on a one-to-one basis, self-observations, or entire workgroups. In some plants this is difficult as there are so few people, so we can also add in 'outcomes' (i.e. the 'What' rather than 'Who'). Whichever approach is adopted has both impact and resource connotations. Second, how often are assessments to be made? Some processes recommend a person do one observation per quarter, per month, per week, per day. The frequency which data is collected is often determined by perceived 'lost opportunity costs' related to a person's time while undertaking observations. Research and common sense tell us the greater the frequency, the greater and speedier the payback (See chapter 5).

Limitless Feedback

The various strands of observation data need to be collated and analyzed so that feedback about performance can be given to the appropriate people. One of the main reasons for a failing process is the lack of means or will to do this. Data lies at the heart of the problem-solving process and it is counterproductive not to use it in the improvement effort. Feedback can be given [1] verbally at the point of observation; [2] graphically with departmental feedback charts; and [3] verbally at briefings where tabulated data is discussed. An important issue is who gets the feedback. In my view, the person(s) or workgroup(s) observed should receive it, although a summary of the entire sites data should also be presented to site management on a frequent basis (e.g. weekly or monthly). They need to be assured that the process is working well and delivering the intended benefits. This also helps them keep their finger on the pulse of the project, which in turn helps to keep them involved and committed.

Assess Current Progress

It is important to stay on top of events if your process is to be sustainable and successful. You should look for the 'tripwires' that could bring your process down. Assessing current progress typically refers to the impact you are making on your stated objectives. For example, although everything appears to be functioning as intended, the incident rates are staying the same or going up. You would have to discover if this is because [a] the targeted behaviors are not focused on injury causing behaviors; [b] because more injuries are being reported as a result of the behavioral process; or [c] because the quality of observations is suspect. Other critical areas to 'keep an eye on' are observation rates, participation rates, levels of safety leadership exhibited and corrective action rates. These are all early warning signals that if left unattended could 'derail' the success of all your efforts. As such, you should be examining these issues on a very frequent basis.

Review and Adapt the Process.

The project team needs to stand back and look at the whole process, particularly in the first two years of implementation. A formal review of the entire process once a quarter is a good idea in the first 12 months, with this 'thinning' to once every 6 months thereafter for the next two years, and once a year thereafter. The review should concentrate on each separate aspect of the process to establish whether they have met their objectives, and whether the outcomes are as intended. In other words, examine the effectiveness of the entire process as a whole, and each individual element. The Behavioral Safety Maturity Ladder in chapter 2 could form the basis for this.

Usually, there will be some lessons learned that can be usefully applied to 'refresh the process' to ensure it becomes sustainable over the longer-term. Some processes have been going for over 30 years or so, while others have fallen at the first hurdle. Those maintained over a long-time period have been nurtured and often expanded into different areas (e.g. Quality, Productivity Environment, Ergonomics, Industrial Hygiene, etc.). Many have fallen by the wayside through neglect, or have failed to deliver because of bad design or application.

Summary

It is evident that implementation of a Behavioral Safety process is not as easy as it first seems. It takes a lot of time and effort to introduce and sustain. The principles outlined here provide a route map to chart a systematic course. Research evidence tells us we must look for deeper issues than the surface behaviors we often see, if we are to understand the 'real problems'. In turn, although focusing on safety related behaviors as the main change agent, we must not lose sight of the everyday realities that drive them. These must also be addressed. The IDEAL process provides a set of practical implementation guidelines, well rehearsed and tempered in the heat of experience.

Many will already be familiar with the concepts of continuous improvement and/or Behavioral Safety. You may already do many of the things presented here. What you may have found is the configuration of what you already have is somewhat different. Perhaps using the principles presented here, you may be able to fine-tune your processes so they deliver bigger and better results.

5 Process Planning

Carol, the safety manager at a Paper Mill had heard about Behavioral Safety at a safety conference. The slick presentation had sold her on the concepts. Her 'take away' was she had to [1] educate people about the psychology of behavior; [2] get supervisors and employees to observe worker activities; [3] isolate target behaviors and [4] get people to challenge each other's unsafe behavior, but praise the safe behaviors observed.

Carol extracted a few unsafe behaviors involved in the Mills incident history. She analyzed them with the Antecedent-Behavior-Consequence (ABC) model and developed a one-hour training presentation on the psychology of safety. Training sessions for all were organized with mandated attendance. After presenting the material, she instructed everyone to observe each other in the work place and identify the common unsafe behaviors. A list of unsafe behaviors was drawn up in each department and posted on notice boards. Everyone had to learn the list, and either praise each other when a safe behavior was observed or challenge each other's unsafe behavior.

Within a week she was receiving numerous complaints. People talked about being spied on by their buddies. Supervisors were playing 'gotcha' and were 'writing people up'. She tried to smooth everything over by explaining it was a new process and some people were bound to be upset, but if everyone persevered the problems would go away and people would not get hurt. Within two weeks, the barrage of complaints had reached a crescendo louder than a Led Zeppelin rock concert.

Bewildered, Carol phoned the Behavioral Safety advisor and told him what was happening and asked for his assistance. She was asked how had she got workforce 'buy-in' and commitment to the process, and how had people been involved in the design and development of the process. Realizing her mistakes, she engaged the advisor. The advisor and Carol apologized to the workforce for not involving people in the development of the process. They asked the workforce to help make the process a success, as it would stop injuries - which was the main aim.

A representative from each department formed a committee. Under the guidance of the advisor, a set of key principles centered on trust and teamwork were developed to establish the ethics of the process. A rollout plan was constructed that spelled out [1] the supporting infrastructure; [2] the integration of the process with existing safety systems; [3] the development of checklists containing a few specific behaviors involved in many injuries; [4] the training of volunteer observers; [5] the deployment of data analysis and feedback mechanisms; and [6] review systems involving everyone. Within a year the injury rate dropped by 49 percent. The workforce was asked if they wanted to continue, with 98 percent agreeing.

The reactions Carol received to her 'home-grown' process are typical when Behavioral Safety processes are done 'at' people not 'with' them. The two missing essential elements were involvement and infrastructure. She at least had the courage to admit her mistakes and move forward, taking the workforce with her. The solution was to form a steering committee to develop the process with the consent and participation of all. This is not the only solution, but it is a common one that has been shown to work.

Creating a Behavioral Safety process is a large undertaking that must be fully understood and planned, *before proceeding*. This increases the likelihood of success by ensuring the appropriate resources are provided and the right atmosphere is created to move forward. Often, this does not happen, and companies are surprised when the process does not meet expectations. Planning generally involves [1] deciding people's roles and responsibilities; [2] deciding on the scale and scope of the process; [3] designing the process; [4] scheduling the roll out; and [5] allocating resources.

The overriding question at each planning stage is: What will make this element of the process a success? Success at each stage increases the likelihood of success at the next. The success criteria can be divided into procedural, staff and 'deliverables'. Collectively these cover [a] the way the process is designed, structured, and managed (Procedural); [b] the involvement and training of the people (Staff); and [c] whether the outcomes of each element are what were intended (Deliverables).

The process can then be evaluated against the success criteria to establish if each element has achieved its aims. At the very least this helps project teams determine the reasons for success or failure at each stage in the process, to ensure there is a firm foundation before proceeding further.

Roles and Responsibilities

Similar to Quality Management project teams, there are many people involved in the design, rollout, execution and maintenance of a Behavioral Safety process. The numbers involved will depend on the number of staff and its scope. In principle, there needs to be recognition that everyone is involved, but each group of stakeholders has a different project role. Exhibit 5.1 provides an overview of typical roles in a well-founded Behavioral Safety process. Each of these roles carries specific responsibilities and accountabilities (the two always go together in life regardless of setting, status, job or activity).

Largely a figurehead on a day-to-day basis, the *Executive Level Sponsor* is the highest-ranking manager possible, in relation to the size and scope of the process. He or she has demonstrable interest in the outcome of the process and is held accountable for success or failure. The sponsor secures the appropriate resources and is seen to visibly champion and support the process. He or she helps to reinforce the legitimacy of the goals and objectives, keeps their fingers on the pulse of major activities on a regular basis, and is t*he* final judge of process related decisions.

The *Executive Level Sponsor* also provides ongoing support for the Project Director and Project Manager and has final approval of all process scope changes. This may include approving each stage of the process, once satisfied the previous stage has met its objectives. Typically, he or she receives monthly progress reports, in terms of schedule, results, and potential problems. The sponsor also acts as the liaison between the project team and the senior management team when developing safety leadership processes.

The *Project Director* is the project champion. A decision-maker, the *Champion* leads the project team (In some instances, the executive level sponsor and director are the same person). Having the same responsibilities as the Sponsor, the Champion also participates in and/or leads the initiation of the process on site. As such this person is actively involved in developing the 'Key Principles' and high-level planning, although it's important the project director avoids managing the team *per se*. Instead he or she is there to guide the project team in its deliberations. The duties could also include approving scope changes, signing off on major deliverables and championing the process with other members of the management team on a regular basis.

It has become evident over the years in many facilities, that *the better the Champion is at the role, the more successful the outcome.* In those facilities where the Champion has become invisible, the process has faltered and in some cases died. Where the Champion regularly asks people about the process during normal business activities, it has achieved remarkable results.

Project Role	Who
Executive Level Sponsor	Chair/ CEO / Operations Director / HSE Director
Project Director	Site Manager / Operations Manager / Safety Manager
Process Coordinator	Site Process Coordinator
Team Members	Project team / Steering Committee
Customers	The entire workforce
Customer Representatives	Workforce observers
Stakeholders	Everybody coming into contact with the process

Exhibit 5.1: Typical Behavioral Safety Process Roles

The *Process Coordinator* is responsible for the day-to-day coordination and management of the process on site (some call these facilitators). There may be a *project coordinator* for each site, or for each business unit on large sites. He or she develops the Project Plan with the team and manages the team's performance of project tasks. He or she also secures acceptance and approval of deliverables from the Project Sponsor and Stakeholders.

The responsibilities are wide-ranging, and include communication, status reporting, escalation of unresolved issues, and making sure the project is delivered on budget, on schedule, and within scope. In some processes, the coordinator takes full day-to-day responsibility for the process and develops sampling checklists, trains observers, collates and analyses data, provides feedback, etc. In these cases, it is important to ensure that everyone knows the coordinator acts with the full authority of the Project Champion. This helps to overcome 'status' problems that might arise from an employee coordinator dealing with managers who are not quite so enthusiastic about the process.

Team Members generally encompass the *Steering Committee* whose responsibilities can be wide ranging. In some processes they are essentially departmental representatives who meet on a monthly basis, passing on lessons learned, unresolved issues or new innovations, etc. In others, they are responsible for implementation. In these latter processes, the roles of each team member tend to be pre-defined. These steering committees comprise of the project director, project coordinator (or facilitator), data entry clerk and/or data analyst, recruiters and trainers of observers, process ambassadors, and drivers of corrective actions. Each person is assigned a role appropriate to his or her skill set, usually for a year. Others are then given the opportunity to take part. Often, team members serve on the committee on a part-time basis.

Their basic responsibilities are to establish key principles, align the process to the company's business needs and culture, sell the process to all, develop sampling checklists, recruit and train observers, collate and analyze data, provide feedback, pursue corrective actions, conduct process reviews, develop a publicity machine, etc. The project director / coordinator will hold each person accountable for delivery to the customers (i.e. the workforce).

Customers consist of the entire workforce. They are the beneficiaries. Every aspect of the entire process is designed and delivered for the benefit of their safety. In turn this benefits them by making their lives safer and reducing injuries. The company benefits from reduced injury costs and improved operational efficiencies.

Their responsibility is to *'use the process'*. This may include attending briefings and 'kick-off' meetings, working safely, being observed in the workplace, attending feedback meetings, highlighting hazards, reporting system or equipment faults and near-hits, taking part in celebrations, suggesting process improvements, etc.

Customer Representatives are the observers. Drawn from all levels of the company, they help to look out for the safety of their buddies, in whatever form that may take. This may simply be providing feedback about safe behavior, coaching of unsafe behavior, reporting hazards or near-hits, following up on corrective actions, etc.

Observers responsibilities include being trained, conducting observations, turning in the sampling checklists on time, holding feedback meetings, helping workgroups set improvement goals, reporting issues back to their workgroups, suggesting process improvements, etc.

Stakeholders refer to anybody who will come into contact with the process, in whatever form, who can impact or be impacted by the process. This may include contractors, suppliers, business customers, visitors, other regions, divisions or sister companies. Try to include 'long-term' contractors in the process from the beginning, as this helps to ensure that everyone on site is in alignment and on the same page.

Project Team Considerations

The above highlights the major roles found within most Behavioral Safety processes. Before starting, think about the configuration of the project team. Many use steering committees, both coordinators and steering committees, or just coordinators.

If you wish to use steering committees, issues to consider will include [1] the use of existing safety committees or creating a committee specific to the Behavioral Safety process. For large sites, you might also consider whether a committee is required in each business unit; [2] the frequency with which they meet; and [3] the scheduling of the process rollout.

If you wish to use a project coordinator (I have mainly used this approach over the past 20 years) you will need to appoint a full-time person who is committed to safety, who reports to a champion. On large sites containing several businesses belonging to the same company, a coordinator has been appointed in each unit. These coordinators report to their respective champions, who meet on a regular basis (e.g. monthly or quarterly) to ensure a consistency of approach.

Some prefer a mix of the two types of teams. They appoint a full-time project coordinator, who is supported by a part-time steering committee that meets monthly. This structure is shown in Exhibit 5.2. In this approach, team members also assist the coordinator during periods of intense activity (e.g. developing sampling checklists, training observers), or stand-in during vacation or sickness absence.

Pros and Cons

The advantages of steering committees are thought to reside in site wide representation and distribution of the workload across many. The disadvantage of most steering committees is their part-time nature: Everything takes so much longer to implement and responsibility for action can become diffused, with important actions 'slipping between the cracks'. Communication within and between steering committees can also be very challenging.

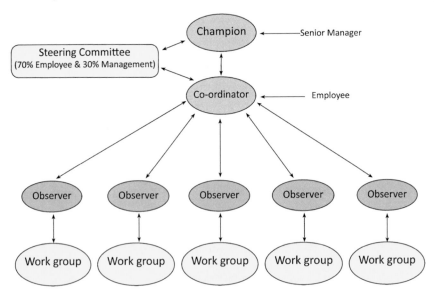

Exhibit 5.2: Example Structure of Project Team Configuration

The advantages of a dedicated two-person project team (project coordinator and champion) are the rapid speed of implementation, with instantaneous decision-making and appropriate corrective actions being made in real time. The disadvantages of a small project team relate to workload, sickness absenteeism, and vacation periods: Alternative cover has to be provided. This is often managed by training two or more coordinators at the same time, with one being appointed to the role on a full-time basis and the other helping out 'as and when' to keep their skills up to speed.

Project Team Training

Regardless of the type of project team chosen, all team members will require training in the principles and practices of Behavioral Safety. This includes the process sponsor, director, coordinator(s), and team or steering committee members, who require in-depth understanding of the process in its entirety.

Most genuine professional advisors tend to include training modules that expand on how to [1] develop and plan the overall process to fit the company's requirements; [2] conduct communication meetings to obtain 'buy-in' to the process; [3] work with all levels of the company to develop people's roles and responsibilities; [4] develop appropriate sampling tools; [5] train observers to use the sites checklists, provide coaching & feedback, and identify 'barriers' to safe behavior; [6] collate, analyze, and interpret observational data; and [7] maintain and sustain the process. Some also include how to help others set improvement targets.

If a steering committee is used, additional training might encompass [1] how to develop a governance document; [2] how to make the best use of time in meetings; [3] conflict resolution; and [4] how to ensure the process maintains its integrity.

Simultaneously, the training period is often used as a vehicle to help the team build their implementation plan. This overcomes the problem of the guys feeling they are being 'lectured' as this requires 'hands-on' use of the materials, which adds value but also requires true expertise on the part of the trainer. The project team training is usually conducted by professional advisors, or 'in-house' experts who have been 'trained as a trainer'. Often, project team members supplement their training with follow-on coaching, attending conferences and/or seminars and, visiting other sites implementing a Behavioral Safety process.

Staff success factors include the project team having a very clear understanding of their role, and of the training content. *Procedural success* could include ensuring all the topics were covered during the training, and transmitted in ways to guarantee understanding (I have been in many facilities where the project team was struggling because the initial training was inadequate and the 'trainer' has moved on). *Deliverable successes* could be defined as the development of an initial implementation plan tailored to the facility.

Key Principles

One of the first actions of a project team is to develop a set of *'Key Principles'* that will guide the ethics of the Behavioral Safety process. Many skip this step, but it does set a useful framework for an ethically sound process, setting the right tone for implementation and reducing potential 'kick back'.

There are many people involved in a Behavioral Safety process who can choose to behave 'ethically' or 'unethically'. These include all levels of management who choose to provide or not, the necessary direction and resources, their intellect, and their demonstrable visible ongoing support. The process champion(s) can choose to actively champion the process or become invisible. The Trade Unions can enthusiastically embrace and support the process, or work actively to undermine it. The steering committee or project team can proactively pursue everyone's involvement in the development and running of the process, or develop it to meet their own political ends by falsifying data and issues. The workgroup observers can observe honestly and openly or can 'cheat' and be 'dishonest' in their recording and reporting of safety performance. And finally, the workforce can actively support or resist the process.

This wide range of participants demonstrates that just one example of unethical behavior from one source could undermine the sterling efforts of everyone else involved. By way of example, one site I worked with had been implementing Behavioral Safety for about four years with very good results. One afternoon, a supervisor 'disciplined' someone as a result of an observation. Written assurances had been given at the start that this would not happen. Within 30 minutes the process had halted across the entire site of 500 people. The only way to revive the process was to dismiss the supervisor with immediate effect!

The 'Key Principles' setting out the ethics of the process should include Trust, Integrity, Teamwork, Involvement, and the notion of a continual improvement journey. Trust and integrity are probably the most important. Everyone must feel confident the process is about continual improvement and that it is not a 'blame game'. There must also be trust between the project champions, project teams, and observers about the integrity of the data. When this is missing, many problems ensue that derail the process. Teamwork and Involvement are based on the notion 'Together Everyone Achieves More'. This enshrines the notion the effort is about creating and maintaining a safety partnership for the benefit of all. The continual improvement aspect informs everyone they are on a journey: The end is never in sight. Some processes achieve a Zero injury rate and people become complacent. They let the process go stale, and all of a sudden.....!

Design the Process

There are a number of design considerations linked to the implementation principles (see chapter 4) and avoidance of failure (see chapter 2). These include [1] implementation approach; [2] scale & scope; [3] observational approach; [4] observation areas; [5] sampling checklists; [6] training; [7] number of observers; [8] contact rate; [9] feedback mechanisms; [10] publicity; [11] sustainability reviews; and [12] scheduling.

Implementation Approach

Reflecting the levels in the Behavioral Safety Maturity Ladder (see chapter 2), there are three fundamental approaches to implementation that will determine the impact on injury rates: [1] top-down; [2] bottom-up; or [3] 'all-inclusive'.

Top-down refers to managerial / supervisory led processes. Du Pont's STOP system is a classic example of this approach. Managers and supervisors observe worker's behavior and give positive or negative feedback to employees. This approach is simple to implement and can have positive effects, *provided it does not become a 'blame and discipline game'.* At the very least, it demonstrates management's commitment to safety and encourages visible safety leadership. The fundamental problem, however, is the workforce are *passive* recipients not *active* participants. Safety is being done 'at' them, not 'with' them. In terms of Behavioral Safety maturity levels this approach would achieve a level 1 or 2. In my experience, this approach has an approximate three-year 'life-cycle' before fading away. On a positive note, it often sets the scene for a 'full-blown' Behavioral Safety process.

Bottom-up refers to employee-led processes. This is probably the most common approach to Behavioral Safety. Employees develop and run the overall process to suit their needs, conduct peer observations, provide feedback and eliminate 'barriers' to safe behavior. Some of these processes have lasted for more than three decades, while others have failed in the first year. The major determinant of success is strong managerial support. If this is not forthcoming, it creates the impression that management does not consider safety as important as other business priorities. In turn, employees turn their attentions to these other priorities and the Behavioral Safety process 'withers on the vine'. In terms of maturity these would achieve levels 3-4 depending on how comprehensive the process was and how supportive management was.

All-inclusive approaches refer to a safety partnership between managers and employees, where all are fully involved and have a clear role to play. Becoming more popular by the day, they actively embrace the notion of team working. Senior managers engage in clearly defined safety support behaviors, line managers conduct observations and engage in clearly defined safety leadership behaviors, checklists are targeted at the safety related activities of everyone in the company, and employees observe the behavior of everyone (including managers), with regular feedback about progress being provided to all. This approach reflects a maturity level 5.

Top-down approaches, though common are not as effective at injury reduction as employee-led process, which in turn are less effective than the 'all-inclusive' partnership approach. Each approach requires significant effort to make them work, but the cost-benefit ratios are significantly different. For a little extra effort, the payback can be as much as ten times greater. Thus, the choice here is how much effort the company is prepared to put in to maximize the benefits: The greater the effort, the greater the rewards.

Scale and Scope

Scale refers to the site(s) and locations within the site(s) where you intend to implement. I would strongly argue against pilot projects *'within'* a business unit. Some will ask 'why us?' others 'why not us?' In other words it can be divisive and can affect later success when you try to roll it out in the areas previously untouched. I have also seen such pilots left to 'drift'. Highly safety conscious, low injury, departments have volunteered to be the vanguard and are three years into the process, while the high injury departments are still sitting back making no attempts to become involved. In my view, it is better to implement across an entire business unit in one go, from top to bottom, to hit the incident rate more quickly. This will not unduly increase resource requirements if the design of the process is optimally configured.

Scope refers to who is to be involved. Again, in my view everyone has the potential for his or her job role to become part of the incident causation chain. Therefore, everyone should be involved (see chapter 4). This not only talks to the Team and Involvement aspects of the 'Key Principles' but continual improvement as well. Paul O'Neill, the former CEO of Alcoa, recognized the financial benefits of full involvement. Safety improvement was one of his major leadership strategies. Why? Because he knew that when a company has got safety right, the spin-offs lead to high performance in many other areas. Some CEO's I have worked with have also subscribed to this view, and have even performed the observer's role in the administration buildings where they work, in addition to their Sponsor or Champion role.

Once these basis decisions have been made, the project team is ready to start designing the process to deliver the maximum benefits in the shortest time frame.

Observational Approach

There are three basic observational approaches: [1] peer to peer; [2] workgroup; and [3] self-management. Some processes also focus exclusively on the 'outcomes' of behavior, rather than people's actual behavior, but these are much less common.

In terms of injury reduction effectiveness, analysis of published scientific research shows 'workgroup' approaches are best, followed by 'outcomes', followed by 'peer-to-peer' (one-on-one). A relatively new approach, no data was available for self-managements, but case studies indicate they can be highly effective.

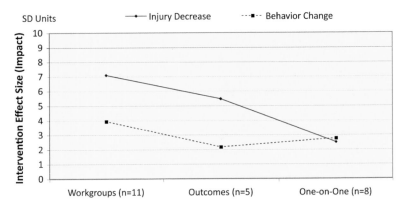

Exhibit 5.3: Effectiveness Comparison of Observational Approaches

The most popular, *'one-on-one, peer to peer'* observations refer to trained observers monitoring an individual for a period of time (e.g. 30 seconds to 2 minutes or more). After observing they provide feedback, praise, coaching, etc., and record the results on their sampling card or checklist, which is 'turned-in' to the project data-entry person. Common Key Performance Indicators (KPI's) are the percentage participation rate and percentage safe.

Typically, the observer asks the person for their permission to observe. If the answer is no they ask someone else. This continues until someone agrees. In my view the 'ask permission' approach often means that only a few people in a facility are actually observed, meaning the unsafe behavior of only a few people is addressed. The remainder carry on as 'normal' in full knowledge they only have to say 'No' if approached by an observer. This may be one of the reasons 'peer to peer' approaches are less effective than workgroup approaches at reducing accident/injury rates.

To make the observers life easier, some processes have the 'guys' place stickers on their hard-hats indicating their willingness to be observed. Unfortunate side effects are those not doing so 'stick out like a sore thumb'. They may be one of the safest workers in the facility, but the natural assumption is they prefer to work unsafely. Instead, they may simply not like someone standing over them distracting them from the job in hand.

Typically, this observational approach requires a lot of time and effort to recruit a sufficient number of observers, or even to get people to observe at all. Many companies have had to resort to quotas and /or inducements just to get observations done.

The next most popular method is the *Workgroup* approach, which refers to one workgroup member, monitoring the behavior of all their colleagues during a single 10-15 minute observation. Feedback is provided at the point of observation, with the sampling checklists turned in for data entry and analysis. In-depth analyses of the workgroup observations are provided as written feedback and presented at weekly team meetings. Group members rotate every few months when checklists are updated. In this way, every workgroup member eventually becomes an observer focused on relevant unsafe behaviors. This approach overcomes much of the resistance to a Behavioral Safety process and is THE most effective method for reducing incident rates.

Self-management refers to employees developing their own sampling checklist and monitoring their own safety performance, and providing their own feedback. Typically, this approach is used for 'lone' workers such as drivers or pipeline walkers, or when the workforce is fearful that the results of observations conducted by others will be used against them. It takes some creativity to obtain and collate and analyze the data, but has shown to be highly effective with the right amount of support.

Before deciding on the observational approach, conduct a quick assessment of the types of activities undertaken in each location: i.e. are they fixed processes with a stable workforce, or are they dynamic settings with transient workforces. Stable workforces in fixed locations lend themselves to a workgroup approach. Dynamic settings with a transient workforce (e.g. construction) or small crews temporarily working in a multitude of locations (e.g. utilities) lend themselves to both workgroup and 'peer-to-peer' approaches. Lone workers (e.g. delivery drivers, sales people) lend themselves to self-management. You may wish to use one method across the board, or a mixture of all three.

One of the *golden rules* of Behavioral Safety is to *'involve people whenever and wherever you can'*. As such it may be a good idea to allow the workforce to decide on their preferred observation approach, as this will help to minimize any resistance. These issues will affect the final process design, so you will want to maximize the benefits by adopting the most appropriate approach in each setting.

Project Team and Observer Recruitment

Consideration also needs to be given to the recruitment of safety observers and project team members. There are three basic approaches: [1] asking for volunteers; [2] mandating everyone participate; and [3] voting for people to be observers.

Obviously one volunteer is worth more than ten pressed men. However, change initiatives are not always welcomed as they can be seen as extra work and stressful. Partly this stems from having to acknowledge existing methods are not delivering as intended. The future can also appear to be uncertain. Therefore some resistance to the change effort can be expected. Exhibit 5.4 illustrates that ten percent of the workforce is likely to welcome the change and ten percent will be vehemently against it. In between these two extremes, 40 percent will be receptive and 40 percent skeptical.

Attempt to recruit the ten percent who are most enthusiastic from the outset. Usually, these people would form the recruitment pool for the project team, and the first wave of observers (assuming there are enough of them). Even so, recruitment can be difficult unless the benefits are accentuated. Generally, this means emphasizing how serious the company is about the process and proving it by completing corrective actions that arise from the briefings, assessments, and data-mining activities, as well as those from the observations once they start. In many ways, this is in the hands of the project team, and given the authority and budget, many will join the project team to test the company's resolve in this regard. If found wanting, the process will die before it even takes off.

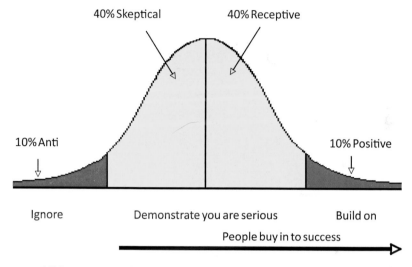

Exhibit 5.4: Normal Distribution Curve of Enthusiasm for Change

If your enthusiastic people can be used to demonstrate the power of the Behavioral Safety process, others will surely follow; usually those who were receptive will jump in next, followed by those who may initially have been skeptical. Those who are 'anti' may remain so. The trick is not to make them 'martyrs'. Try and address their concerns (they may have good reason for being anti), but don't keep pursuing them. If you keep paying them attention those who were skeptical to begin with, will follow. You could then find the whole process unravels. In other words, whoever makes the loudest noise wins. If the company can prove by its actions (not words) that it is serious about the process, 90 percent or more of the workforce will become involved.

Another approach is to mandate participation. On this basis people will be chosen, unless volunteers come forward. There is mounting evidence to show this has a bigger impact than a voluntary approach. Some of the Oil companies I have worked with have mandated participation, but followed up with 'who wants to go first'. This achieves a balance between the voluntary and conscript approaches.

In Asian cultures, it is common for people to be selected by their peers and 'voted' in as a project team member or observer. In some instances an 'election' may need to be held.

If you are not sure which approach is best for your company, it is a good idea to list the advantages and disadvantages to each method and base your decisions on the outcomes.

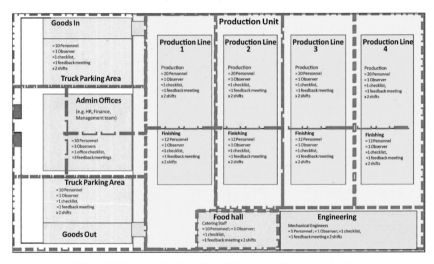

Exhibit 5.5: Example Site Map Showing Observation Areas

Identifying Observation Areas

To foster 'area ownership' within a facility it is a good idea to identify observation areas. Workgroup approaches should conform to a workgroups 'normal' working area. A 'peer-to-peer' approach may also benefit from an area ownership approach, as it may provide opportunities for a single observer to monitor several employees during the observation period.

The principles of identifying observation areas are relatively straightforward. Either obtain the facility's site map, or create one. As shown in Exhibit 5.5, divide each business unit into its Departments and Work areas. Determine if the observer can walk around the entire area in the allotted observation time and draw a dotted line around the identified area. If adopting a workgroup based approach, the site map will also allow you to determine the number of observers and the number and type of checklists required.

Sampling Checklists

Many of the popular 'peer-to-peer' type processes use a single sampling checklist to cover the activities of everyone on an entire site. Others (myself included) start with the assumption you need different sampling checklists for different activities.

Single sampling checklists can literally be 'blank cards' to cover a multitude of behaviors in all sorts of circumstances, or generic cards with a set of pre-determined categories (e.g. PPE), which contain sets of general 'catch-all' behaviors (e.g. Head, Arms & Hands, Trunk, Legs & Feet). The problem with blank cards is their lack of focus. For them to be effective, the workforce must train to recognize safe and unsafe behaviors. Often, people are unaware that certain behaviors are unsafe. The problem with generic 'catch-all' cards is that they do not focus on the 20 percent or so repeat behaviors implicated in the lion's share of incidents.

Developing different *sampling checklists* refers to developing checklists for particular job tasks or locations. This makes much more sense than a single checklist for the entire site, as different jobs contain different activities that represent different risks. For example, administrative work requires different sets of behaviors than operating a crane, which are different again from working at heights. Data mining of your incident database (see chapter 6) will highlight particular categories of behaviors causing concern. If you do this by location (as recommended) you will identify problem behaviors by department, work areas, job, task, etc. It is these you should use to develop your sampling checklists (see chapter 7) as those focused on specific incident causing behaviors lead to faster and longer-lasting incident reduction.

If you adopt a specific checklist approach, use the site map to determine the number of different checklists needing development. It is likely you can use the same checklists across the different shifts in a single area, or across areas using identical production processes. Be guided by the different activities represented by each area.

Don't forget to include sampling checklists for administrative functions (e.g. Human Resources, Purchasing & Supply) focused on the activities that could cause safety problems for others somewhere else in the company. Similarly, a good process will recognize the need to develop managerial support checklists (in conjunction with users).

Training

There are three aspects to Behavioral Safety training: [1] who is to be trained and when; [2] its content, which needs to focus on both [a] technical and [b] process issues; and [3] scheduling & medium.

People

All levels of management will require training in safety leadership and process support activities. The entire workforce will require an overview of the process and their role, and observers will require training in observation, feedback and coaching skills, leading safety meetings, and setting improvement targets.

Content

Training should include an overview of the Behavioral Safety process to enhance their understanding of the underlying principles, how Behavioral Safety works, and how the process will fit with the company's existing safety efforts. This will enable the project team to 'sell' the process to others.

The technical aspects for observers and safety leaders include the use of the appropriate sampling tools, how to conduct observations, give verbal feedback, and coach others.

Scheduling and Medium

Other considerations will include the timing, length of training and venues, and the appropriate mediums to use. These can include documentation, videos, slides, workshops, and individual coaching.

Training Success Criteria

Key success criteria would include [1] attendance; [2] each attendee understanding their respective roles in the process and supporting it; [3] being able to use the appropriate sampling tool; [4] being able to provide and receive 'useful' verbal feedback and coaching. You may want to consider professional assistance to meet these requirements.

Contact Rate

Data sampling frequency is known to determine the degree of incident reduction. The more frequent the better (See Exhibit 5.6). Some processes advocate daily sampling per observer, others 2-3 times per week, while others suggest once per week, per month, or per quarter. Each approach has resource implications. Many of the less frequent contact rates arise from perceived 'lost-opportunity' costs by supervisors of shift managers. Equally, there is sometimes a lack of willingness on the observer's part.

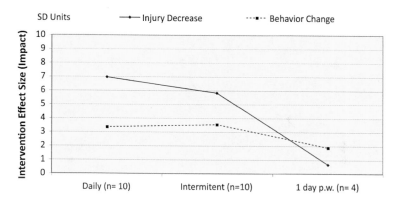

Exhibit 5.6: Effectiveness Comparison of Contact Rates

It is important the project team provide clear guidelines on the contact rate issues to clarify everyone's expectations. This is easier for workgroup observation and self-observation approaches. Both can maintain a 100% daily contact rate with little effort or extra resource.

Peer-to-Peer approaches are not quite so simple. The number of observers recruited largely dictates the contact rate in these approaches. Some Behavioral Safety advisors suggest 20% of employees are observed weekly. Some 'User' companies mandate that 'everyone' be observed at least once a month. Both of these imply there must be a sufficient large number of trained observers to maintain these contact rates. In many cases this means *the entire workforce* has to be trained as rapidly as possible.

Feedback Mechanisms

Feedback is the key to performance. Many processes rely solely on immediate verbal feedback at the point of observation. Others use a combination of verbal feedback and analysis of the entire sample of checklists turned in. However, these analyses are often given to the steering committees rather than the workgroups or work areas the data was generated from, if it is analyzed at all. Those that do take the time and trouble to collate and analyze their data can use it for graphical representation of progress and also produce 'fine-grained' feedback of the safe and unsafe behaviors performed by a particular group of people. This can be discussed at weekly team meetings to provide collective knowledge of what is being performed well or not so well, so people can adjust their behavior accordingly.

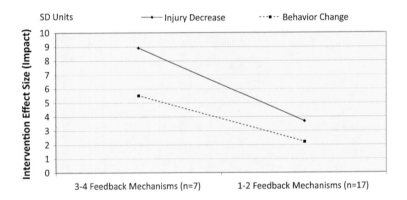

Exhibit 5.7: Effectiveness for the Number of Feedback Mechanisms

Research evidence shows Behavioral Safety processes should use as many feedback mechanisms as possible to reduce injuries and benefit from potential cost savings. However, the resource implications include the cost of meetings (though existing departmental meetings and tailgate talks could be used), graphical feedback charts, and the purchase or development of software with which to collate and analyze the data. All these resource costs are 'small potatoes' compared to the cost of just one lost-time injury.

Publicity and Marketing

Most process will require some form of publicity or marketing campaign to complement the introduction and maintenance of the process (see chapter 9). This helps to obtain and maintain 'buy-in', ownership, and commitment. In terms of process implementation, conduct briefings with all departments and shift crews and inform them about the entire process, what it means to people individually and collectively and ask them whether or not they will support it. At the end of the meeting, ask people to identify safety problems and log and deal with them 'As Soon As Is Practicable' (ASAP). The idea is to demonstrate how serious the facility is about improving safety. Publicizing what has been accomplished every step of the way is one of the key methods to maintain the observation process. Publicizing such 'fixes' maintains everyone's enthusiasm and keeps people involved. Delivery mechanisms include regular newsletters, meetings, computer intranet web pages, etc.

Briefing

'Staff success' could be defined as people understanding why the process is being introduced, how it works, and how it will impact them. *Procedural successes* could be defined as 95 percent of kick-off briefings being held with 95 percent of site personnel attendance. *Deliverable successes* would include [a] the majority of the workforce being willing to support and become involved in the process; [b] people volunteering to be either project team members or observers; [c] a number of previously unknown safety problems emerging that require corrective actions.

Branding

A common initial activity is to ask people to 'name' or 'brand' their process, to emphasize the process is new and something different. Our process is called B-Safe®, and many clients use it and our logo in a slogan such as 'B-Safe at.......'. This works on many levels, for example, it is [1] an instruction (B-Safe out there); [2] communicative (work safely in this facility); [3] a constant reminder for everyone to work safely; and [4] provides a recognized anchor for the process and related improvement activities. In the example below, we were careful to link the process to the main safety management system to highlight the fact the process was integrated into the main safety management system (RGEE), and was not a passing fad. With no lost-time incidents over 136 million man-hours by the end of 2008, it appears to have met all its objectives.

General publicity for the process can also be achieved by other means. For example, communicating the key principles on posters, developing individual and group celebrations for achieving milestones, developing safety awards, competitions, slogans and logos, small group discussions, holding annual Behavioral Safety conferences, having safety day celebrations, incorporating knowledge of the process into site inductions, etc.

Sustainability Reviews

There are two kinds of sustainability reviews: Fine-tuning in light of ongoing progress and formal process reviews.

Fine-Tuning

Fine-tuning the process can happen in many ways. If you set some Key Performance Indicators (KPI's) for the process, and monitor ongoing progress against them, non-conformance will soon be detected and the appropriate action taken.

Another example may be changing the checklist behaviors. For example, use of hearing protection may have started at around 35 percent safe and you are now achieving a constant 95 percent safe score or above. Change your checklist and target another significant problem behavior. Too many times I have seen steering committees devoting all their time and effort to ensure a 100 percent safe score on a behavior that is already scoring 97 percent safe. Meanwhile all around them other high injury potential unsafe behaviors are occurring that are not on the checklists. In these instances, the process has become a 'numbers game' with no real focus on continual improvement.

Formal Process Reviews

This refers to making ongoing adjustments to the process as you achieve milestones. These should be planned for and built into the process schedule. Typically, these start 3-6 months after 'kick-off'. In the first year, I would recommend one formal review per quarter, just to make sure the bedrock of the process remains solid and the process 'stays in lane'. In the next 24 months reduce this to once per 6 months and in the fourth year and beyond, once per annum (unless major changes indicate otherwise).

The reviews should cover the implementation of the entire process to identify improvement opportunities. This includes the performance of the project team, the resources available, the levels of managerial support, the design of the checklists, the observation process, data entry and analysis, publicity communications and the customer's perspective.

Scheduling

Having developed a plan accounting for your preferred process design, schedule the activities so progress can be evaluated against a timeline. The decision here is how aggressive you want the schedule to be. Many managers expect to see immediate results and are not impressed with 'slow' rollouts that increase the time to impact.

Depending on the approach adopted, the implementation schedule can be relatively short (3 months) or quite long (up to 12 months or more). With the strong assistance of a great HSE team, advance preparation and a lot of hard work, I once implemented a workgroup approach with 10,000 Nigerians and 10,000 third-party nationals on a large LNG construction project for Shell in just 17 days! I'm told the project eventually achieved 37 million man-hours without a lost-time incident.

Try to ensure the 'rollout' schedule does not coincide with other change initiatives. Develop 'milestones' for achievement, by which each component or feature must be developed and implemented. Many Behavioral Safety initiatives have come unstuck because there was no schedule to help structure the process.

The typical implementation schedules of many peer-to-peer approaches range from 6-12 months before trained observers are 'on-the-ground'. Workgroup approaches can typically be up and running within 12-16 weeks. Self-observation approaches can be implemented within 2-4 weeks. Obviously these time frames are dependent on the number of people on site and their availability.

Following the continual improvement process cycle in chapter 1, typical activities include:

1. Assessment and delivery of report
2. Site briefings about the process
3. Project team training
4. Checklist development
5. Managerial alignment
6. Observer training
7. Establish Baselines
8. Set improvement targets
9. Provide feedback
10. Review and adapt
11. Repeat from 3 or 4.

Summary

Creating a Behavioral Safety observation process is generally a large undertaking and should not be approached lightly. The real keys to success are planning, structure, communication, involvement, and resourcing. Involve everybody as much as possible in the detailed planning and development process, to facilitate ownership of, and commitment to the process. Similarly, ensure the appropriate resources are available. An under-resourced Behavioral Safety process will be difficult to implement and maintain. These can be identified by considering the Behavioral Safety model to adopt, the number of observation areas, the number of observers, the observational approach, the frequency of observations, and the time frame for action.

6 Locating Safety Problems

A multi-national company had spent $52 million dollars introducing a new safety leadership initiative. Every manager had received training to observe and intervene when a worker acted unsafely. 'Safety is a line management responsibility' and 'all injuries are preventable' was constantly impressed upon everyone. Three years later, Rob, the Vice-President of Operations, was concerned the money was ill-spent as serious injury rates had risen year on year. He realized something was wrong, but did not know what or why. Managers corrected unsafe behaviors, safety officers provided safety training, Safety Committees were in place, all serious incidents were investigated, and those experiencing more than one injury received 'counseling' about their poor safety attitudes.

After assessing his options, Rob hired an independent company to review the situation and advise him on the way forward. A comprehensive assessment strategy was drawn up that included an HSE survey, incident database analyses, site observations and a safety management system review. Rob chose the five sites with the highest injury rates for the review. The survey was distributed to every staff member and employee. During the survey period, each site's incident database was examined for common themes. Armed with this information every site was visited and people's 'on-the-job' behavior observed. The reviewers also sat in safety committee meetings and 'shadowed' managers as they did their walk rounds. They then examined the safety management system in each facility in terms of its design, reach, and effectiveness. All the data was compiled and analyzed to provide a written report with recommendations for action.

Uncomfortable reading, Rob found the results disturbing. They revealed that managers sincerely believed they were showing a strong commitment to safety, whereas employees thought otherwise. It was apparent the company had a 'sanitization' culture where near-hit reports and minor incidents were filtered out of the system if a supervisor or manager looked bad. Inconsistency was also the order of the day, as managers scolded employees one day for unsafe working, but next day encouraged them to 'break' the safety rules if behind on production. Injured employees were consistently blamed for their injuries, given written warnings and fired if they sustained three. Safely documentation was comprehensive, but access to it was limited and people did not really know what was in it. Adaptations to safety manuals also had to be 'signed off' by every senior manager on site. Treated as a single document, they were forced to read the entire manual. Overall, the review revealed the majority of people found safety was 'punishing'. This led to the 'real' safety problems being driven underground, which only surfaced when a serious incident occurred.

Cultural Assessments

Locating problems often means assessing a company's safety culture to get at the behavioral, system, and person factors affecting safety performance. Misunderstanding the wider culture can lead to a failing Behavioral Safety process. In the case study, it was easy to spot the 'fear' culture, which led to the 'blame' and 'sanitization' sub-cultures. These types of culture can seriously dent a Behavioral Safety process. A blame culture often means employees won't even attempt to engage in the process for fear of being 'punished' in some way. Fear cultures often lead also to 'falsified' data just to make everyone look good: A prime example of a tendency for people to put their social safety before their physical safety. The value of a cultural assessment is to ensure a goodness of fit between the design of the intended Behavioral Safety process, its implementation and day-to-day reality.

Cultural assessments involve an examination of the practices that are impacting on safety performance from a variety of viewpoints. A good assessment will target people's views about safety, their everyday safety behavior, and the effectiveness of the management systems: the three major inputs of safety culture.

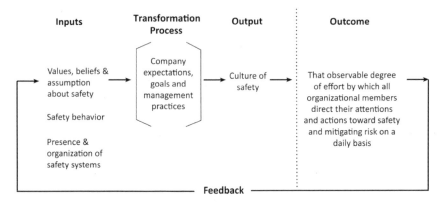

Exhibit 6.1: Business Process Model of Safety Culture

The Business Process model of Safety Culture (see Exhibit 6.1) uses these three input factors to illustrate that the *'Inputs'* are *'processed'* by a combination of the company's goals and management practices and *transformed* into the safety culture *'Output'* to create the safety culture *'Outcome'*. How a company manages the safety 'Inputs' determines people's commitment to safety and actual performance. All of these are important to Behavioral Safety processes.

Objectives

In practical terms a cultural assessment helps to establish the best process design and implementation strategy by identifying potential obstacles to success. These examine each of the inputs and the company's goals and managerial practices. The purpose is to help build an effective and sustainable Behavioral Safety process by recognizing strengths and weaknesses that will support or hurt implementation. Often, because of the specialist skills involved, large-scale assessments will require professional assistance.

Planning

Cultural assessments require careful planning that centers on [1] what is going to be assessed; [2] how it is going to be done; [3] what the outcomes are; and [4] what is considered a successful outcome. These considerations help to focus the assessment, increase its effectiveness, and provide in-depth information to facilitate the design of a successful Behavioral Safety process.

What is to be Assessed?

Many companies believe an assessment comprises *solely* of a survey of employee's perceptions about safety. This is a very limited view and a more holistic approach is desirable if the Behavioral Safety process is to hit all the *'hot spots'*. This can be seen in Exhibit 6.2, which presents a company's safety culture profile compiled from assessments focusing on Process, People, and Actions.

The profile identified areas of opportunity to more fully integrate a Behavioral Safety process at the 'Operational' level by increasing managers' involvement, and improving the corrective action systems at the 'Defensive level'. In this case, the two most fundamental aspects for improving a safety culture (leadership & action) were identified as being the weakest. By triangulating the assessment methods, a more complete picture of the issues was obtained. This helped in targeting specific areas where the impact would be greatest, to sustain the existing Behavioral Safety process and improve the overall safety culture.

Organization Level	Process	People	Actions	Risk
Strategic (Execeutive Decision makers)	79%	80%	80%	Medium
Operational (Line Management)	66%	62%	87%	Medium
Tactical (Support Functions)	82%	84%	86%	Medium
Behavioral (On the Job)	94%	91%	88%	Low
Defensive (Risk Controls)	85%	47%	40%	Medium
	81%	73%	76%	

Average Score = 77%

Exhibit 6.2: Example Safety Culture Profile

Assessment Tools

Available tools to assess each input element include [1] incident database analyses and site observations to identify key safety behaviors and other related issues; [2] perception surveys and Focus Group exercises to discover people's values, beliefs, and assumptions about safety; and [3] system reviews and interviews to examine the Safety Management Systems impact on people's safety behavior. Addressing the 'how' of assessment, decisions about which tools to use and the scope of assessment will influence the outcomes for each set of activities and the accompanying *process progress* and *outcome success* criteria.

Assessment Strategy

The assessment strategy should target each of the physical site locations where Behavioral Safety is to be introduced. Multiple location assessments are obviously much more comprehensive in scope, but the assessment principles remain the same.

The assessment strategy should also focus on each layer of the accident causation chain: from people at the strategic level through to those running the defensive systems, whether in one or more locations. Capturing senior managers views, behaviors, and the policies/systems they operate under is equally as important as capturing everyone else's.

Evaluating Progress

Assessment progress should be evaluated against a pre-determined time schedule. What is to be assessed and how it is to be done will shorten or lengthen the schedule accordingly, although 'slack' needs to be built in for 'no-shows' and vacation periods. Each of the activities should be scheduled from start to finish, creating a common platform of understanding for all involved. This also helps to identify logistical issues such as who needs to be *where* and *when* with *whom* to complete *which* aspect of the assessment.

Assessment Deliverables

The *deliverables* from each assessment method should be specified before the assessment begins. These provide an evaluation benchmark to determine the success of the assessment. For incident database analyses this would mean identifying the small proportion of behaviors responsible for the lion's share of the facilities incidents. The findings would be tested 'on-site' from observations to assess their validity and identify other common 'unsafe behaviors'.

For surveys these would include identifying [1] people, process, and action issues that will support a Behavioral Safety process; and [2] barriers to implementation. Focus Group exercises would identify what the current problems are, what people want to improve, and specific action plans to get them there.

System reviews would build on the previous two assessments to identify [1] which aspects of the site's management systems were driving the unsafe behaviors identified in the incident database analyses; and [2] where the 'barriers' to safe behavior are being caused by the systems.

In combination, these will determine the causes of injuries *and* if the conditions are appropriate for proceeding with Behavioral Safety.

I have often asked companies to address certain issues prior to implementation. All have gracefully acquiesced; in full knowledge the result would be a much smoother and longer lasting process to help achieve their incident reducing objectives.

Locate the Problem – Data Mining

The start point for an assessment should be *data mining* to extract *hidden* patterns from injury databases. Some company databases merely record incidents and calculate incident rates, with their use restricted to recording and reporting, rather than being used as a tool to get to the underlying issues. The vast majority of safety professionals look at the frequency of particular incident types, but not all try to look beneath the surface of the entire data set.

Data mining is a method to make better use of existing data, by sorting through to identify patterns and establish relationships so it can be used to *predict future behavior.* I developed and use PinPoint™, a propriety data-mining method to locate and predict the likelihood of a particular category of behaviors triggering an incident. This makes use of all types of incident data from a multitude of sources (e.g. near-hit reports, recordable and reportable injuries) and establishes the relationships between them. Once the initial analysis is completed it is maintained to provide an ongoing 'real-time' profile that helps focus observations.

The easiest way to start is to examine the site's relatively recent incident history (two years or so) by physical location (e.g. department). Some use 3 to 5 years of incident data. In each location, the incidents are divided into the type of incident causes (struck by, electrical, etc). Drilling down again to identify the injured part of the body helps to identify particular tasks and the specific behaviors involved. These are categorized into common themes (e.g. body positioning, use of tools, etc) and charted so the relative importance of each becomes visible. It is a good idea to develop control charts (i.e. calculate the mean and spread) to highlight those categories above the upper limit, as this will be where the major problems lie.

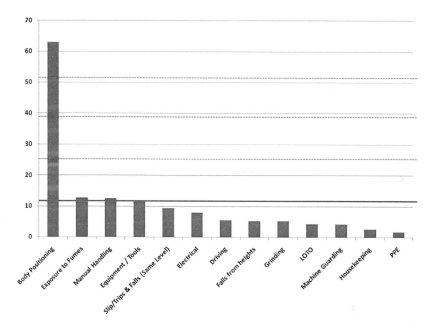

Exhibit 6.3: **Incident Profile and Control Chart**

The example PinPoint™ profile in Exhibit 6.3 identifies 'Body Positioning' as the major issue, with a 63 percent chance of an injury occurring. The significance is confirmed by the upper control limit (dotted line) being breached. Other areas of immediate concern would be the next two categories from the left above the mean (Exposure to Fumes and Manual Handling). Those on or below the mean (solid line) are also issues that need addressing, but with lesser priority than those above the mean.

Validation Check

Examining the original incident reports (if available) helps to guide site observations to validate the data-mining results. If your analysis is correct, you should 'see' many of the injury causing behaviors being performed. The site observation also allows you to see the unsafe behaviors in context, in terms of the tools and equipment being used, the layout of the workplace, and the sequencing of activities. Other related unsafe behaviors may also come to light that have previously been overlooked.

During these site observations, it is also worth examining the supervisory arrangements, production schedules, and any machinery 'downtime' rates to assess their likely influence on unsafe behavior. The idea is to discover other issues driving injury-triggering behaviors. In one factory, I discovered that a combination of sickness absenteeism and machine 'downtime' was the major driver of over half the injuries. Resolving the machine downtime problem alone would have helped to reduce incidents by 40 percent.

Clearly and concisely recording your findings is important. The example below (Exhibit 6.4) uses common Quality Management categories found in 'Fishbone' problem-solving diagrams (i.e. Management, Manpower, Methods, Materials, and Machinery) to provide structure.

Injury Catagory	# of Injuries	Management	Methods	Materials	Manpower	Machine
Body Positioning	63	Increased production targets by 20% to meet customer demand	Operators reaching into machine to clear products, while presses are closing	Raw material (rubber) sticks to surface of press	All operators	Presses are faulty, but put into operation to meet customer demands
Exposure to fumes	12		Fume cupboard bafflers often blocked with apparatus	Storage items placed behind the person's workspace interups airflow	All Laboratory technicians	Fume cupboard doors not being closed properly

Exhibit 6.4: Example Site Observation Record

At a glance the record should show what the issues are in each category. In the example, at the behest of a customer, management has increased the production targets by 20%. Second-hand machines were put into operation to meet customer demands, despite them being faulty. Raw material (rubber) sticks to the presses after product is removed. This and the faulty presses cause 20% of the product to be non-conforming. Operators attempt to reduce waste and re-work by removing debris sticking to the presses, *while the presses are closing*. Thus a specific unsafe behavior has been identified (for use at a later date when developing sampling checklists). The simple solution here is to refurbish each machine as quickly as possible (perhaps on a rolling basis). Eliminating the 20 percent of defects will enable the company to meets its production targets, without people being injured: A win-win situation. If the faulty presses are not attended to, the behavior of reaching into the machine will not stop, and any Behavioral Safety process will have little, if any, effect (apart from annoying everybody).

On the other hand, the 'exposure to fumes' example reveals all the issues are behavioral. The placing of apparatus inside the fume cupboard blocks the bafflers, the storage of materials is interrupting airflow, and the fume cupboard doors are not being pulled down properly. These are all behaviors within people's immediate control that can easily be addressed with a Behavioral Safety process. The '5 Why's' questioning technique is a simple and effective method to understand the reasons for these types of behavior. Alternatively, 'Applied Behavioral Analysis' is a more formal method to identify the triggers (antecedents) for these three unsafe behaviors and the reinforcing consequences to the person. In either event, the purpose is to help identify appropriate solutions.

Data mining and validation checks can provide the foundation to help focus the development of all other assessment activities (and observation checklists at a later date). Many do not go to these lengths, but I am a firm believer in making Behavioral Safety decisions based on data (it is one of the reasons for a successful 20 year track record).

Locate the Problems - Seeking Peoples Views

It is important to seek people's views about safety to help ensure the Behavioral Safety process is optimally designed and will be well received. Employee input from a wide range of staff allows you to identify strengths and weakness in the way safety is currently being managed in many business units, and develop specific ways forward for each, that will support the implementation.

Surveys

Developing a safety survey is a mixture of art and science requiring a high degree of skill, experience and thorough training. Many professional Behavioral Safety companies possess specialists with these skills who have developed their surveys. The focus of these most often reflects the particular advisor's approach to Behavioral

Safety. Some are geared solely toward Safety, some Safety and Behavioral Safety, while others are more general and focus on Organizational Culture *per se*. Most survey employee's views of Management's Commitment, Managerial Actions, Communications and Safety Training, the four topics currently *known to predict* actual levels of safety performance. Low scores on these four topics are associated with high incident rates.

Quality Standards

The accepted quality standards to establish the worth of safety surveys are reliability and validity.

Reliability refers to the *consistency* of measurement over multiple distributions. It is the 'yardstick' indicating a survey is a stable measure of people's perceptions. The *minimum* Reliability Coefficient considered acceptable is 0.70. That is, the survey will reliably measure people's safety perceptions 70 percent of the time. However, you would not want the county assessor to measure your plot acreage for taxes with a ruler that is only 70 percent reliable! Likewise, you do not want to purchase a survey that is only reliable 70 percent of the time. The results could send you down the wrong road entirely and cost you a lot of time, money and effort! Thus the higher the number the better, somewhere above 0.90 is ideal (absolute perfection is 1.0 and is generally unattainable with perceptual measures).

Validity refers to the *accuracy* of measurement. It is the 'yardstick' that confirms the survey is measuring what it claims to measure. There is *face validity*: It looks like its measuring safety (but that does not necessarily mean it is). There is *content validity*: The questions truly represent the domain of interest. For example, measuring management's commitment to safety means asking a few questions about the type of things management does to improve safety. There is *concurrent validity, which* refers to the strength of association between the survey *scores and actual safety performance* (generally incident rates). Providers usually refer to concurrent validity when describing their survey. Finally, there is *predictive validity*: The survey scores predict actual and future safety performance (e.g. incident rates, levels of safety behavior). Focusing corrective action on low scoring predictive topics will lead to substantial increases in safety performance.

Predictive validity is the most important property of a survey, as the coefficient is directly proportional to its practical economic value. The *predictive validity coefficient,* therefore, provides a marker of the potential financial value of that survey to your company. Most predictive validity coefficients are small, ranging from 0.20 - 0.35, with coefficients above 0.50 being extremely rare. Squaring the coefficient gives an indication of the actual overlap between the survey scores and safety performance. For example, 0.50 means there is a 25% overlap (0.50 X 0.50 = 0.25 X 100). In many companies, a 25 percent improvement in safety performance equates to cost savings of hundreds of thousands of dollars.

Benchmarking

Many (but not all) providers offer to benchmark a company's scores with all others in their database (or a chosen sub-set) to provide a comparison. The underlying idea is to shift corporate mind-sets from relative complacency to a strong sense of urgency for ongoing improvement, once the company is aware of how its performance compares to its peers. Benchmarking can be within an industry sector or across a range of industries.

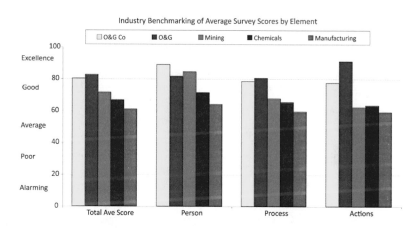

Exhibit 6.5: Example External Benchmark

Some present the results as percentile scores. For example, if Company A's scores on management commitment reached the 90th percentile, it means their scores are better than 90 percent of other management commitment scores contained in the providers database.

Though common and market led, one problem with this approach is that not all companies are alike, even within the same industry. For example, the surveyed company might have experienced industrial relations problems or cutback on maintenance because of financial difficulties (which tend to lower the scores) and benchmark companies did not. This could inflate small differences into larger ones that do not really exist.

A more useful approach is internal benchmarking, where survey results of departments are compared against other departments, and/or managers' perceptions are compared to those of frontline employees. This approach highlights the best and worst scoring business units and provokes discussions about the reasons for the differences, leading to appropriate corrective actions. Progress can also be tracked across time if surveys are conducted annually.

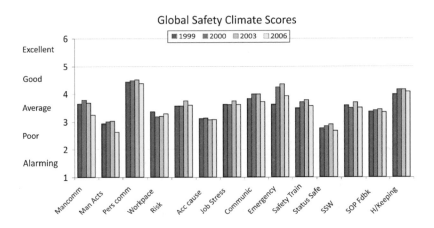

Exhibit 6.6: Example Internal Benchmarking by Year

Because of the very close relationships between safety, quality and productivity, safety survey results also tend to signal the effects of changes in other areas of a company's activities. This can be seen in Exhibit 6.6 where the management commitment and managerial action scores significantly worsened in 2006 compared to previous years. The company concerned was going through turmoil at the time, with management focusing on issues other than safety. In turn, this created more negative perceptions about safety in almost every other area. This demonstrates that safety survey scores are sensitive to changes or problem issues in non-safety areas. Thus, internal benchmarking is a much more valid approach, where apples are compared with apples, rather than external comparisons potentially comparing apples and oranges.

Digging In

Responses to individual questions should also be presented as percentages of those who agree or disagree to a question. These form the basis for discussion and corrective action at worker feedback meetings. If you get a similar response to the question below, you know many believe productivity generally comes before safety. This will influence the effectiveness of your Behavioral Safety process.

	Agree	Disagree
People stopping work on safety grounds know they will get the support of supervision	28%	72%

To overcome this, it makes sense try to obtain an agreement from management that they would support anyone stopping work on safety grounds. Perhaps by reminding them the small advantage gained from making a few more 'widgets' could be heavily outweighed by the costs of an injury and the associated downtime. If that agreement is obtained, it could appear on safety leadership checklists (see chapter 7).

	Grouping	Agree	Disagree
The company's use of Trichloroethylene is dangerous to workers health?	Managers (110)	17%	83%
	Operatives 400)	93%	7%

Comparing managers and frontline employee's responses also helps prompt discussions to assist in the creation of the safety partnership, which in turn will help with the sustainability of the Behavioral Safety process.

Focus Group Exercises

Another method to obtain employees views about safety is to use Focus Group exercises. More flexible, these can be used to complement or be used as an alternative to surveys. Focus Group exercises are designed for people to participate in a *guided discussion* about a particular issue. During the exercise, facilitators should focus on the issues surrounding the high injury categories identified from the data-mining.

A good structure is provided by the Cultural Web, which provides eight specific elements for people to collectively explore the company's safety issues. These are:

- *Routines* – How is safety routinely managed?
- *Rituals* – How does your company reinforce the importance of safe behavior?
- *Stories* – What messages are transmitted by employee's stories about safety?
- *Symbols* – What symbols are used to communicate the importance of safety to employees?
- *Power* – What beliefs about safety does the company's leadership hold and how does this translate into practice?
- *Safety Structures* – What formal and informal safety mechanisms are in place?
- *Safety Controls* – What does your company measure, monitor, and reinforce to drive safety performance?
- *Underlying Assumptions* – What is the company's underlying safety philosophy?

Delegates use these elements to identify '*where they are now*' in relation to safety by using a series of questions within each element. This prompts employees to explore the way safety is currently practiced and reveals how safety in the company is *really* perceived by employees. Although their perceptions may differ from expectations, these are constantly being reinforced by the way the company's underlying assumptions about safety are manifest in day-to-day life.

The results are summarized, capturing every group's views, to provide a representation of 'taken-for-granted' aspects of safety. Often presented in visual form, the results show the links between behavioral, symbolic, structural, and political aspects of the company's safety efforts. As such, they provide a strategic overview of the values, beliefs, and assumptions that are guiding safety on a day-to-day basis.

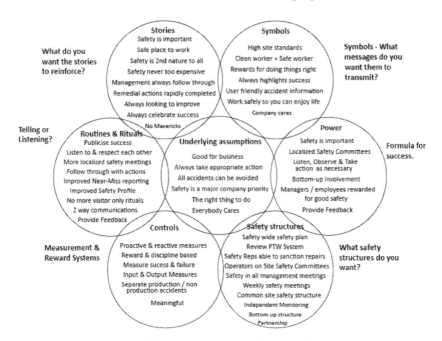

Exhibit 6.7: Example Cultural Web

The Cultural Web findings are used as a prompt for employees to identify what aspects of safety they desire to improve the current situation. The *'gap'* between *'where you are now'* and *'where you want to be'* provides the basis for action plans and the route to achieve them. This provides a clear picture of specific factors for change. Participants then prioritize the actions by effort and impact. Analyses to identify the forces that will work in favor of, as well as against change are also useful.

ACTIONS	PRIORITY / IMPACT
Monthly safety talks to be conducted during the day, not on night shift	Easy / High
EHS to provide common safety library in Control Room	Easy / Low
More time to be given for effective shift handovers	Difficult / High
Safety and Loss Prevention Department to be one department	Difficult / Low

Exhibit 6.8: Example Actions Arising from a Cultural Web Exercise

The Focus Group exercises can also be conducted departmentally with the results usefully compared to identify strengths and weaknesses. Guided by the initial incident analyses, it should be possible to identify appropriate action plans to eliminate the drivers of the small number of behaviors responsible for the lion's share of incidents. It is also possible to compare the values, beliefs, and assumptions of high and low injury departments. The differences would form the basis for discussions and action to bring the high injury locations on the same plane as low injury departments.

Locate the Problem - System Reviews

System reviews are intended to examine the situational aspects of safety to assess their influence on day-to-day safety management. These can range from annual audits by internal and/or external auditors of every aspect of the system to more focused assessments of particular components. Whichever approach is adopted the intention is to examine the design, reach, and effectiveness of the system.

The system *design* will often mirror legislative requirements, though many companies go beyond these. In broad brush-strokes most Safety Management Systems will mirror the design and the associated activities in Exhibit 6.9.

SMS levels	Org. levels	SMS Components
Policy	Strategic (Excecutive Decision-makers)	Leadership, Commitment, Accountability
Organizing	Operational (Line Manangement)	Risk Assessment & Risk Management
Planning & Implementing	Tactical (Support Functions)	Human Resource, Procurement, Engineering, Safety, Facilities Design
Measuring Performance	Behavioral (People & Systems)	Operations, Third-Party Services
Reviewing Performance	Defensive (Risk Control)	Incident Investigation & Analysis, Maintenance, Management of Change, Information & Documentation, Operations Integrity& Improvement, Community Awareness & Emergency Preparation

Exhibit 6.9: Example Safety Management System

Using this example Safety Management System as a guide, it is possible to examine the situational drivers involved in the high injury categories identified during the data-mining process. It is also possible (though unlikely) that a company's Safety Management System does not have the majority of components in place. Comparing the Safety Management System manual with the example would quickly identify any 'gaps'.

The *'reach'* of the system refers to knowledge about the system and its use. Examinations would ascertain if people know about the system and which aspects of it apply to their job role. Questions might focus on the availability of the system documentation to the job holder, whether it is to hand, whether it is understandable, whether it applies to their job role and whether it is used, and if so, how often. For example, does the system direct purchasing and procurement to assess the impact of their intended purchases on safety, prior to purchase. In one company, an operator was covered in Sulfuric Acid. To save a $10 charge for each order from the supplier, the purchasing officer double-ordered without asking the operators how much product was already in the tanks. The supplier arrived on site and began filling the tanks. Before he had finished with the second half of the load, the overflow valve vented product all over the area, splashing an operator who suffered severe chemical burns from head to toe. This cost the company a small fortune in compensation and regulatory fines.

System *'Effectiveness'* refers to its impact on people's daily working lives. Does the system influence operations on a daily basis? Is it aligned with other systems such as quality and production? Do people follow the policies and procedures? Are people held accountable? Is the system adaptive to day-to-day activities? For example, one facility experienced work interface problems: A crew working at heights was working above another crew working on the ground. Both crews had been granted a Permit-to-Work and were authorized to be in their respective areas. Fortunately, one of the crews recognized the hazardous nature of events, stopped work and returned the Permit. This caused major productivity problems, which were discussed later that day at a management meeting. It soon became apparent the Permit Issuer was losing track of permits issued. Putting a site map on the wall in the Permit office, and placing a colored pin in each location where a Permit had been authorized resolved the problem. The idea being a cluster of pins would signal potential interface difficulties. This very simple but effective solution was rapidly incorporated into the

Permit-to-Work system documentation, a good example of a system's effectiveness and adaptability.

In principle, the results of the injury data-mining process are used to identify 'broken' aspects of the safety management system. Focusing on these 'broken' aspects and drilling down helps to discover the major situational drivers of the injury triggering behaviors.

Certainly a high frequency of injuries in any category should prompt a review of the risk assessment, risk management, and risk control process surrounding the tasks involved. For example [1] reviewing whether the jobs / tasks involved have been risk assessed; and [2] examining if the results were used in a meaningful way to improve Standard Operating Procedures, or if physical layouts were re-designed, etc. If they were used, it may prove useful to examine the knowledge of the jobholders to discover if they know about the risk assessment and any changes to operating procedures or the job flow process. If they don't, it signals poor communications. British construction sector research found poor communications was implicated in 50 percent of all fatalities! If people do have the required knowledge, it could be worth examining the system for conflicts with the quality and production systems. Other issues worthy of examination include job planning, management, manpower levels, methods, machinery, and materials, etc.

From a slightly wider perspective, it may also prove valuable to examine the effectiveness of safety committee meetings, tailgate talks, managerial walk rounds, safety inspections, record keeping, and shift handovers. These are all activities that can reinforce the importance of safety or otherwise, depending on their effectiveness.

Bringing it all Together

If you have used all the assessment methods described here, you will have obtained a very comprehensive picture of your company's safety strengths and weaknesses and hopefully developed some very specific actions plans. It will also give you a good view of your current safety culture.

The findings should be written into a report detailing the way forward, that includes a brief explanation of the assessment methods used, the major findings, and recommendations. However, it is important to do this on two levels: [1] strategically for the assessed location(s) as a whole, which is presented to senior management; and [2] tactically for each department or business unit in that location, which is presented to the 'local' management and employees.

Strategic Report

The report is both a factual 'State of the Nation' address and a marketing presentation to obtain senior management support for the chosen way forward. The strategic overview of the findings should be short, sharp and to the point.

1. The reason we did the assessment was ……
2. The assessment methods / processes were …….
3. The location(s) involved were …….
4. The major findings are ………..
5. The way forward is ………….
6. The estimated costs / benefits are ……………..

Senior managers are very busy but talented people, and are used to receiving summaries. They will dig deeper into the issues if they so choose (be prepared!). It may be a good idea to 'bounce' the report off your 'local friendly senior management representative', to ensure the report has the right 'balance and tone'. In my experience, senior managers of a company are highly committed to safety. They are usually very disappointed when everything in the garden is not as rosy as they had been led to believe (remember all those visits where senior managers were given the royal tour!) and want to quickly put things right.

Tactical Reports

Reports for the individual locations or business units should present the data that is specific to them. This could also include an internal benchmark against other business units. It should certainly highlight the way forward and why, and the resource implications (if known). Again, get the report 'checked' by a 'friendly' manager to ensure it strikes the right tone and balance. Strident, 'scare-mongering' reports put people on the defensive. When that happens, they often go into denial and rejection. The goal is to successfully bring about the desired change.

Place the specific corrective actions obtained from each assessment method in the appendices of the report, so it provides the means to track progress. These should also be themed and prioritized.

Permit to Work	Priority
1. Quality of standby persons to improve	High
2. PTW procedure to be simplified	High
Emergency Equipment and Procedures	
1. No pre-warning when fire drills are going to be practices	Low
2. Head count procedures in case of an evacuation, to be reviewed	Medium
Personal Protective Equipment (PPE)	
1. Stores to have sufficient amounts and sizes of PPE at all times	High
2. Replace faded PPE sign boards	Medium
Housekeeping	
1. Increase waste collection points	High
2. Increase storage space of warehouse	Medium
HSE Training	
1. More persons to be trained on JSA's	High
2. First aiders to receive refrest training	Medium

Exhibit 6.10: Themed and Prioritized Corrective Actions

Following through on the corrective actions is most important. It will help to create the right atmosphere for implementing a Behavioral Safety process, help create (or maintain) the safety partnership, and build support for other safety efforts.

The report should be followed up with a presentation to as many people in the business unit as is practicable. If you have used assessment methods that involve everyone, they will already have some idea of the issues and corrective actions, but a formal presentation helps to build support for the recommendations. You need their 'buy-in' to any improvement initiatives and it is also courteous to give feedback to people who have been involved in providing the information. Discussion of the findings also provides an opportunity for further engagement in the improvement process. The presentation should be more detailed than that presented to senior managers and should list the strengths of current safety efforts, the weaknesses identified, the proposed solutions and any identified barriers.

Summary

Locating problems that are driving unsafe behaviors requires a comprehensive, systematic, and structured assessment. There are a number of tools and methods that can be used, each one shedding light on the issues from different perspectives. At the very least these should focus on Person, Behavioral, and Situational issues. A thorough assessment will help to overcome any obstacles that may hinder the implementation and sustainability of your Behavioral Safety process.

Consider using professionally developed safety surveys to assess people's perceptions about safety, as there is significant amount of expertise and skill involved. If you do use one of these, ensure it has *predictive validity* so you can assess the likely financial value-added to your company.

7 Sampling Tools

An industry magazine was interviewing Tom, an ethylene plant safety officer for nearly 30 years, about his experiences of involving people to help improve safety. Collecting his thoughts, he ran through the site's history. After learning of a catastrophic incident in a similar plant to his own, he had begun with a 'near-hit' reporting system. Introduced with great fanfare, Tom recalled he had received 23 reports in the first month. Primarily these had focused on people driving too fast in the parking lot, though one or two focused on steam leaks or tripping hazards. Within 7 months the process had died. On asking why people didn't participate, he learned people were fearful of being blamed because of the 'shoot the messenger' culture.

Tom had then tried a Hazard ID scheme. This worked for a short while, but again faded away. Tom discovered operators were required to fix the hazards they found, without extra pay for the additional work. The 'guys' then simply stopped reporting hazards. He devised a scheme where the guys could report both unsafe behaviors and unsafe conditions on a blank form. Initially, none were received, so he mandated everybody would receive credits for the numbers they turned in, that they could spend in a catalogue. This worked. People were handing them in. A few reported serious plant issues, but most were about people not wearing their PPE or leaving doors open, etc. He had got involvement, but three years later, the incident rate remained unchanged.

Realizing people needed extra guidance about the type of things to look for Tom had used the Internet to obtain copies of various observation cards. He found one that pretty much covered everything under the sun. Calling it 'Safe Acts', Tom trained the guys to use it to record people's safe or unsafe behavior. He encouraged them to give praise when people were observed working safely, or coach those working unsafely. He also encouraged them to record people's reactions to being observed, and any unsafe conditions that required attention. Over the next couple of years, he saw a 15 percent decline in injury rates.

One day he came across a Behavioral Safety web site. This said 'the more specific the behaviors on a checklist, the bigger the impact'. He decided to contact the company & asked them to help him refresh his current process. Together they identified the current injury triggering behaviors in each site area. They met with a large number of the workforce to discuss the behaviors on the checklists to seek approval. The guy's were also asked how they would like to see the process work. The workforce eliminated the need to record people's reactions. Within a year, the incident rate dropped by 45 percent. Within two years, the site achieved a zero incident rate, which has since been maintained. He told the interviewer the major lesson was to seek guidance, focus on specific problems, not to try cover everything all in one go, and get the guys to help with everything. With good advice & complete involvement, an appropriate process can be devised.

Over a number of years, Tom learned that eliminating a safety problem requires real focus and involvement. His sampling tools started out with a very broad scope and eventually became much more focused. He found the more specific the sampling tools became, the bigger the impact they exerted on the incident rate. Another lesson learned was to involve people in the development of the tools and their 'rollout' at the outset so potential *'tripwires'* could be avoided.

Exhibit 7.1: Drilling Down to Focus on Important Issues

In a sense, Exhibit 7.1 reflects the 'maturity' of a Behavioral Safety process (see chapter 2). Those processes only using near-hit reporting systems are giving birth to a fledgling Behavioral Safety process. They are asking people to be involved in the safety effort by observing and reporting instances of near-injuries (i.e. something happened, but by the grace of God nobody got hurt). Hazard Identification systems are Behavioral Safety processes learning to walk and talk. They begin to focus people's attention on potential equipment failures, the wider working environment, and the man-machine interface. Behavioral Safety Processes using 'blank' cards are like teenagers. Unfocused the resulting observations swing wildly from one thing to another with no discernable effect on the real issues. Generalized observation cards are like undergraduate college students. Focused on a wide range of issues, they only scratch the surface of a topic. Those Behavioral Safety processes utilizing focused cards or checklists are akin to mature and productive members of society. They achieve what they set out to achieve.

In combination, near-hit reporting, Hazard Identification, and focused Behavioral Safety checklists provide a very powerful set of safety tools. One type should not be abandoned in favor of another. Near-hit reports capture random moments of near-disaster, and can uncover previously unknown unsafe behaviors or unsafe sequences of behavior. Hazard Identification focuses attention more on Process Safety issues and highlights potentially catastrophic failures related to the integrity of plant and equipment. They can also identify ergonomic issues related to the behavior of people when interacting with machinery and equipment. The findings from either of these methods can help to focus the Behavioral Safety checklists. In turn, these can help to focus hazard-spotting exercises and make people aware of specific behaviors that can result in injury. Thus, each complements the other.

Good Behavioral Safety processes collect and integrate data from multiple sources to facilitate performance monitoring and analyses to drive continual improvement. A behavior sampling tool is just one of a number of tools in the 'safety toolbox'. Cleverly used in an integrated way, the impact is much greater than the sum of the parts.

Data Types

The types of data required for monitoring a Behavioral Safety process will drive the development of the appropriate sampling tools. Typical data types and their collection include trained observers sampling their colleague's ongoing safety behavior using safety behavior checklists. The frequency of safe and unsafe behavior in their area of work is recorded, and a Percent Safe score calculated. This observation process can also help to identify unsafe conditions. Less commonly, managers provide weekly self-observation data of their safety related activities. These are used to calculate a Percent Safety Leadership score. Some processes also include specific safety leadership observation cards for managers to use during field observations. Visible Ongoing Support checklists are used sometimes by observers to indicate the amount of support received from managers, supervisors, project teams, and employees.

Project team members also use incident and near-hit data to drive the focus of their Behavioral Safety process. In addition they can collect and/or track data on the number of people trained to be observers, the identified number of training needs, the number of feedback meetings held, and so on. The engineering function can provide data on the number of corrective actions complete or incomplete. This is not an exhaustive list of who collects data or the different types, but does illustrate the wide-ranging nature of data collection within a good Behavioral Safety process.

Types of Behavioral Safety Checklists

The most common sampling tool in a Behavioral Safety process is the safety behavior checklist. By and large there are three basic types: job specific, generic, and outcome focused. Regardless of type, they should target very specific behaviors or outcomes to maximize the impact. This also overcomes the need for long lists of 'operational definitions' commonly found in many processes.

Job Specific observation checklists contain multiple categories of specific safety behaviors that reflect specific safety aspects of a specific job or task, performed in a specific work area (e.g. personnel are removing the key when leaving a parked forklift truck). Shown in Exhibit 7.2, Job specific checklists are often developed and used for those jobs or tasks with a high risk of injury.

Other forms of job-specific checklists relate to the safety related activities of support functions such as Purchasing & Supply, Human Resources, Engineering, Safety, Health & Environment, etc. These focus on specific activities known to impact on the safety of others (e.g. I checked training records to ensure people had received refresher training on forklift trucks, etc). People self-monitor themselves against these on a weekly basis, with the results collated and analyzed in the same way as the safety behavior checklists.

Category 1 : WORKING AT HEIGHT	Safe	Unsafe	N/A
1. When using scaffolding, personnel are			
1.1 Using ladder access only (not climbing the scaffold frame)			
1.2 Working with their bodies inside the handrails			
1.3 Using a hand line to hoist & lower materials &			
1.4 Keeping the decking clear of materials, equipment & debris			
2. Personnel are only using scaffold displaying a Green Scafftag			
3. When there is a fall of more than two metres & a safety harness is being worn			
3.1 The harness is properly fastened and adjusted			
3.2 The lanyard is tied off to a strong anchor point			
Percentage Safe = (Safe / Safe + Unsafe) * 100			

Exhibit 7.2: Example Job Specific Checklist

As well as attempting to cover the job functions at each of the five levels in the Accident Causation chain, these types of checklists also provide opportunities to begin linking Behavioral Safety into the company's overall Quality Management process, its strategic goals (e.g. Purchasing and Supply Management (PSM) change), and Supply Risk Management chain. Exhibit 7.3 provides an example job specific checklist for the Purchasing & Supply function that is designed to eliminate frequent Human Errors in Patient Safety.

Category = Purchasing Patient - controlled Analgesia Pumps	Yes	No	N/A
1. I limited the purchase of PCA pumps to a single model			
2. I checked the pumps can be programmed easily to deliver the desired concentrations			
3. I checked the PCA pump could not allow accidental use of free-flow			
4. I checked the pump operation is easy to use for both clinicians and patients			
5. I checked drugs, units of delivery and strengths appear in a logical sequence			
% Safe = Total Yes /(Total Yes + Total No) X 100 Totals			
Comments			

Exhibit 7.3: Example Purchasing Specific Checklist

Generic checklists contain multiple categories of safety behaviors that are generic to many site work areas (i.e. Personal Protective Equipment, Housekeeping, etc.). More readily accepted because they are less threatening to people, these are often developed and used in the initial stages of a Behavioral Safety process, or when the workforce is skeptical. Shown in Exhibit 7.4, each category contains a number of specific behaviors that are generic to a specific work area (e.g. personnel are wearing hard hats, gloves, eye protection, etc).

Category 1 : PERSONAL PROTECTIVE EQUIPMENT	Safe	Unsafe	N/A
1. Personnel are Wearing			
1.1 Gloves			
1.2 Steel toe-cap boots			
1.3 Safety glasses			
1.4 Hard hat			
Category 2: HOUSEKEEPING			
2. Personnel are			
2.1 Keeping walkways clear of rubbish & debris			
2.2 Coiling hoses after use			
Percentage Safe = {Safe / Safe + Unsafe } * 100 Totals			

Exhibit 7.4: Example Generic Checklist with Specific Behaviors

To some, a generic checklist means generic sets of behavior rather than specific behaviors within a generic category of behaviors applicable to all. Exhibit 7.5 tries to cover everything within a category. This type of checklist will require a separate list of operational definitions, and people will require a lot of training in its use to ensure they understand what it is they are observing.

Generic Observation Checklist	Safe	At Risk	Comment
PPE			
Eyes / Face			
Hearing			
Hand			
Foot			
Protective Clothing			
Housekeeping			
Slip / Trip			
Storage			
Egress			
Total			

Exhibit 7.5: Example Generic Checklist with Generic Behavior Sets

In my view one of the success criteria for a checklist is that anybody can pick it up and immediately know and understand what behavior is to be observed, simply by reading it. Comparing the two types of generic checklist makes this clear. In Exhibit 7.4 in the Housekeeping category there are two explicit behaviors: Keeping walkways clear of trash and debris, and coiling hoses after use. In the same category in Exhibit 7.5 people are being asked to observe a multitude of behaviors under slip/trip, storage and egress. Which one do you think will have the most impact?

Outcome based checklists contain multiple categories of behaviors that reflect the results or outcomes of behaviors (e.g. Use of Cranes, Stacking Pallets, etc). For example, hoses left lying on a walkway. The hose could not get there by itself. The hose left lying across the walkway would have to be the result of someone leaving it there. This type of checklist is often used when it might be very difficult to observe people actually doing something, because people are few and far between (e.g. maintenance workers on a petrochemical plant), and it is easier to observe the results of what people have been doing.

Category 1: PALLETS	Safe	Unsafe	N/A
1.1 No pallets are leaning against walls			
1.2 Pallets are stacked no more than 8 high			
1.3 Pallets are stacked neatly, 'corner to corner'			
1.4 Pallets are not stacked in front of fire exits			
1.5 Pallets are not stacked near a heat source			
Category 2: CRANES			
2.1 Chain hooks are not hanging in walkways			
2.2 Electronic crane control pad is hooked away on wall			
*Percentage Safe = (Safe / Safe + Unsafe) * 100* Totals			

Exhibit 7.6: Example Outcome Specific Checklist

If constructed correctly, Behavioral Safety checklists are both a communication tool and a sampling tool. They transmit knowledge of specific behaviors to people and provide the means to monitor the frequency of safe and unsafe behavior.

Developing Behavioral Safety Checklists

Development of checklists is a systematic but relatively simple process. Tom illustrates many skip this step and copy or purchase one from elsewhere. This is a false economy, simply because these will not be targeting issues specific to a facility, and despite all the time, money, and effort of implementation the impact will be minimal, compared to what could be. Remember the saying; *if a job is worth doing, it's worth doing well!* Development does require time and effort, but the rewards usually exceed expectations.

The development process tends to follow a specific sequence of [1] identifying unsafe behaviors; [2] defining safe behaviors; [3] assigning the safe behaviors into categories; [4] writing the behaviors; [5] developing a recording format; and [6] reviewing and refining the checklists. This is usually done for each business department or work area in a location. In many Behavioral Safety processes, the identified unsafe behaviors are further analyzed to identify antecedents & consequences. This often requires the project team to observe the behaviors in the workplace and talk with people or interview the injured person.

Identifying Unsafe Behaviors

A good checklist 'targets those unsafe behaviors known to be causing injuries in a facility'. This should be used as *THE definition of success* for developing a Behavioral Safety sampling tool. The best place to identify these is in the company incident database. Using data-mining techniques (see chapter 6) the idea is to identify the small proportion of behaviors involved in the lion's share of the incidents. I recommend making use of the previous two years incident reports, as it is more likely to reflect current operational practices. I also don't recommend making much distinction between a lost-time or minor incident. Often, it is only by sheer luck the latter is not the former!

Once identified, the behaviors triggering injuries are assigned into their respective categories (e.g. Body positioning, Welding, Grinding, etc.). If your incident database contains relatively few, there are other sources for identifying high injury potential behaviors. These include [1] the workforce (either from the site assessment, briefings or brainstorming sessions); [2] Risk Assessments or Job Safety Analyses (JSA); [3] Task Analyses; or [4] Standard Operating Procedures (SOP's). In these cases the definition of success is the targeting of behaviors with high injury potential.

Defining Safe Behaviors

The unsafe behaviors identifed need to be converted into 'safe' behaviors, *prior to writing the behavior on a checklist*. For example, a slitting machine is used in the paper industry (and others) to cut rolls of paper or product to size. The slitting knives are extremely sharp discs, sitting on a slitting bar with a spindle through their center. Once positioned correctly, these are 'locked' in place on the bar. Operators often store spare slitting knives on their machines to cater for changing product requirements during a shift. Operators do not know these requirements until they start on a particular order. Many operators have been injured reaching for spare 'slitting' knives they have placed on the right hand side of the slitting bar.

The identified unsafe behavior would be storing the knives in a position (right-hand side) that required someone to reach over and unintentionally place their arm or hand against the slitting knives already in use. The 'safe' behavior could be defined as:

'People are storing spare slitting knives on the left hand side of the slitting bar only'.

We may also wish to restrict the number of slitting knives stored on the machine to avoid further hazards. So we would define another safe behavior as:

'People are storing three knives or less on the machine'.

We now have two safe behaviors defined that *are based on the assumption people are behaving safely*. Because they are based on previous injury history, a postive change in these two behaviors has the potential to reduce or eliminate all the incidents associated with cuts from slitting machines (which is exactly what happened in the factory concerned).

People do not go to work and think 'I will behave unsafely today'. Most of the time, most people behave safely at work, because they want to go home in one piece. This is acknowledged by focusing on the positives when developing sampling tools. It is also another means to overcome potential 'kick-back' from jobholders. When written, the behaviors should also be specific to one activity, clearly observable (by anyone simply reading the sampling tool), and action-orientated. These four features of a checklist behavior provide the means to evaluate the quality of the checklists.

Defining Behavioral Categories

Most Behavioral Safety sampling tools contain various categories of behaviors (e.g. Use of tools, Body Positioning, Access to Heights, Housekeeping, etc.). It is a good idea to use the same categories on the checklists as those used previously in the data-mining exercise, as this will make it much easier to determine the impact of the Behavioral Safety process on incident rates as the process unfolds.

In some processes I have been involved with, the categories referred to areas of the plant, or particular operations. This can be a useful method if most of the incidents in a particular department are limited to one or two physical locations (see exhibit 7.7).

The main purpose of dividing the behaviors into categories is [1] to make the tool easier to use for observers, [2] to facilitate ongoing analyses of the observation data throughout the monitoring phases to ensure relevant feedback; and [3] to facilitate comparisons against behaviors involved in subsequent injuries that may occur in the same topic area. In other words, exploring to see if the behaviors involved in an incident after starting your process are related to any of the behaviors you are already monitoring.

I have seen processes dramatically reduce incidents for a year or so, only to see minor first-aid injuries steadily increase again, simply because the project team have not taken the time and trouble to compare the behaviors involved in these with those on the area checklists. A sustainability issue (see chapter 9), updating the checklists in light of ongoing incident experience is important. The ultimate success factor of the checklist is its ability to increase the frequency of particular safe behaviors, while simultaneously reducing the frequency of injuries involving its corresponding unsafe behavior.

Writing the Behaviors

The behaviors should be written with a single focus in mind. In the following example of a behavior from a 'real' checklist there are actually three behaviors. *'Inspect and make sure a tool or equipment is not defective before using it. Never use defective tools or equipment. Return these for repairs or discarding'.* Not only could these be viewed as a set of rules or procedures rather than behaviors, they could also create difficulties in scoring, which in turn affect data analyses and feedback.

In my view, it would be better to separate these into individual behaviors. For example, [1] people *are* inspecting their tools for defects before use; [2] people *are* not using defective tools; and [3] people *are* returning defective tools for repair. In this way, the observer is recording whether each one of these is performed safely or not. It may be (and often is) the case that people perform two of these safely, and one unsafely. Thus, another success factor in checklist development is that each behavior is focused on only one activity.

Research shows sampling tools containing more than 20 behaviors are less effective at injury reduction as the sampling becomes too superficial for the observation time allotted. A rule of thumb therefore, is to ensure that the sample tool is no longer than one page (inclusive of room for comments).

Keeping the number of behaviors to 20 or less, also forces developers to focus on the small proportion of behaviors causing the lion's share of incidents. In this way, the impact will be maximized. Behaviors on sampling tools can always be changed as the current ones are consistently recorded as 'Safe'.

Developing a Recording Format

There are a number of recording formats used in the various Behavioral Safety processes. These range from rating scales and point systems, to those counting the frequency of safe and unsafe (or at-risk) behaviors. The latter is the most common, but all formats attempt to do the same thing: calculate a percent safe score from the safe and unsafe behaviors observed.

I believe it is also a good idea to use a 'Not Seen' or 'Not Applicable' category so that those behaviors not seen during an observation can be recorded. These are monitored by the project teams to highlight the behaviors that occur few and far between. Over a period of time, if they are consistently scored as not seen, they can be removed from the checklist and replaced with another behavior.

Category = Reactor Floor

	Safe	Unsafe	Not Seen
1.0 All personnel using stairs are:			
1.1 Holding handrail with one hand			
1.2 Taking one step at a time			
1.3 Walking not running			
2.0 Personnel are placing filter screens in storage racks			
3.0 Personnel are keeping the reactor bund grids free from waste product			
4.0 Personnel are isolating the reactor before opening the centrifuge doors for cleaning			
5.0 Personnel are barriering off the hoist area during lifting operations			
% Safe = Total Safe /(Total Safe + Total Unsafe) X 100 Totals			

Comments

Exhibit 7.7: Example Plant Area Specific Checklist

Many also record comments. In my view these should be used to record hazardous conditions or identify previously unknown unsafe behaviors. Unfortunately, many checklists contain mechanisms to indicate the observed person's 'reactions' and what they said. Couple this with the location, time of day and other such data recorded on these types of checklist and the potential to identify an individual becomes apparent.

In my view this is highly counterproductive. It is imperative that people feel 'psychologically safe' when involved in a Behavioral Safety process. Creating a genuine 'safety partnership' is difficult when the process becomes a 'blame game'.

Reviewing and Refining the Checklists

Following the golden rule, of *involving people whenever and wherever you can*, the draft checklists are given to the workforce in the appropriate site locations for their review. In essence they are being asked to confirm that the behaviors contained in the checklist are relevant to them. It is a good idea to highlight the number of injuries associated with each one of the behaviors when presenting them to people, so there is little doubt about the reasons for their presence. Often slight modifcations are made to the wording, or additional behaviors are added, replacing those occurring less frequently. Once reviewed, it is a good idea to ask people to field test them. This helps to remove any ambiguity in wording and the average time taken to observe all the items can be determined. If it takes more than 10-15 minutes, it could be worth eliminating behaviors associated with the least number of incidents.

Safety Leadership Checklists

The benefit of managerial *safety leadership* is its impact on employee's safety behavior, which in turn impacts the incident rate. Research has shown the impact of safety leadership behavior is between 35-51 percent, depending on the industry sector. Management's visible and demonstrable safety leadership is, therefore, vital to a Behavioral Safety process for two reasons. Firstly, management's commitment to any improvement project will determine employee's behavior and commitment to the process, and its ultimate success. Second, the co-operation of management is often needed to implement corrective actions that have been identified by employees. In many Behavioral Safety processes, safety leadership is treated as a separate 'add-on' feature. In my view, it should be an integral feature of the entire process from the outset.

Managerial Levels

It is important that all levels of management demonstrate their safety leadership from the most senior managers downward. In Behavioral Safety processes this means defining particular safety leadership behaviors and developing 'self-managed' safety leadership checklists. Managers self-monitor their actual behavior against these, usually on a weekly basis. The checklists are returned to the project team so that they can be collated and analyzed, so feedback about overall safety leadership performance can be provided. In general, it is useful to develop separate checklists for senior site management teams, line managers, and supervisors. Ideally, there would be some overlap between the three types.

Development

The key to developing appropriate safety leadership checklists is to involve people. This is usually achieved by asking managers to attend a session to brainstorm sets of possible leadership behaviors that will support safety in general, the Behavioral Safety process in particular, and be aligned with other company safety objectives (e.g. reviewing the Permit to Work violation log book).

This can be done separately with groups of senior managers, line-managers and supervisor, or all together, with each group on separate tables. Brainstorming together at the same time offers the major benefit of everyone cross-sharing their ideas at the end of the exercise, which leads to better alignment between the three levels.

Safety Leadership Behaviors	Yes	No	N/A
Category 1: People Support			
1. I undertook an 'Operations" safety walkabout			
2. I discussed safety with employees			
3. I asked people what I could do to make them safer in their work			
Category 2: System Support			
4. I discussed safety as the 1st item on every meeting agenda			
5. I reviewed the number of all incident types per asset			
6. I met Asset managers to ensure closeout of corrective actions			
7. I actively supported the closeout of identified concern areas			
8. I tracked the timely closure of process related Root Cause Failure Analysis			
9. I reviewed the Permit to Work (PTW) violation log book			
Category 3: Training Support			
10. I conducted / promoted safety related coaching			
11. I reviewed the status of the competency training			
Category 4: Behavioral Safety Support			
12. I reviewed weekly progress of the Behavioral Safety process			
13. I attended a weekly Behavioral Safety feedback meeting			
14. I coached observers to complete daily Behavioral Safety observations			
Total			

Exhibit 7.8: Example Senior Management Safety Leadership Checklist

Good safety leadership checklists contain categories of behaviors to cover People Support, System Support, Training Support, and Behavioral Safety Process Support (see Exhibit 7.8). Other categories could include Prioritization for Safety, Safety Partnership Involvement, Leadership Observation and Feedback, Communication, Organization, Appreciation, and Resourcing. The main point is to develop behavioral categories suitable for a site's particular safety leadership activity.

Often, there is only a need to develop one checklist for each layer of management, with everyone at each layer using the same checklist. This facilitates the collation and analyses of data across all work areas on a 'like for like' basis. However, developing different checklists for each person is also valid.

Writing the Behaviors

In the same way as the behaviors are written for the safety behavior checklists, the leadership behaviors should be specific and focused on one action. The major difference is that they are personalized to the extent each behavior starts with the first person singular, 'I'. For example 'I reviewed the site's corrective actions'.

In many facilities, clients have developed similar checklists with only ten behaviors, and called them *'The Ten Commitments'*, or *'The Ten Commandments'*. Managers like to have fun too!

Visible Ongoing Support Checklists

Visible Ongoing Support (VOS) checklists are a demonstration of the 'safety partnership' in action. These provide a 'quality' check on the overall support levels received each week by 'Behavioral Safety' observers. In essence, because these can become 'political' if not carefully constructed, it is better they focus purely on the *contact* between managers, the project team, employees, and the observer. Exhibit 7.9 provides an example currently used by one company.

Visible Ongoing Support	Yes	No	Don't know
Category 1: Senior Management Support			
1. A Senior Manager met with and encouraged you in your BBS role this week			
2. A Senior Manager attended your weekly feedback meeting & reviewed BBS data with your workgroup			
Category 2: Team Leader Support			
3. Your Team Leader attended your weekly BBS feedback meeting this week			
4. Your Team Leader met 1 on 1 with you this week to offer support			
Category 3: Supervisors Support			
5. Your Supervisor attended your weekly			
6. Your Supervisor met 1 on 1 with you this week to offer support			
7. Your Supervisor held a discussion on your safety observations this week			
Category 4: Behavioral Safety Support			
8. Has anyone from the Behavioral Safety project team contacted you to ask if they could be of assistance to you this week			
Category 5: Workgroup Support			
9. Did any of your colleagues act on your feedback this week			
10. Did your colleagues discuss the observation results at the weekly feedback meeting			
Total			

Exhibit 7.9: Example Visible Ongoing Support Checklist

Although the monitoring of VOS can have political implications, the scores need not be made public knowledge (though senior site management teams often want a summary VOS score to compare against the safety leadership summary score). They are designed primarily to provide the project team with information about potential problem areas, and as such are a feedback tool.

Summary

The basic purpose of behavioral measurement is to make an improvement, otherwise it is wasted effort. Sampling tools are the 'cornerstone' of any Behavioral Safety process that are used to help direct peoples attention and actions onto behaviors known to be important. There are various types (e.g. Safety, Leadership, Support), but each one should focus on very specific behaviors. They should not be designed to fix 'everything in one go', otherwise the facility could end up doing a lot of things badly, instead of a few things well. In other words, wasting time, money, and effort. Collectively, the data from all checklist types is collated and analyzed and used to provide a basket of 'leading' indicators of safety performance to the workforce and managment teams.

8 Rollout and Execution

Tabitha a full-time academic had read about the behavioral approach and was keen to try it. She contacted various companies and hit the jackpot. She had been engaged to advise a food company that had heard about it at safety conferences, but wanted to do it as cheaply as possible: A marriage made in heaven.

Tabitha recommended starting small on two lines in the production hall for 12 months to learn the lessons and then rollout the process to everyone else. She provided a generic safety checklist obtained from an academic study, and trained half the guys from each shift on its use. They were to show the rest of the shift crew how to observe.

Some of the employees complained it was unfair for them to be picked on and used as guinea pigs for an experiment: their incident rate was no higher than other shifts. Tabitha told them they were special and should be proud of what they were doing, as they would lead the way for the other shifts. Somewhat pacified they did the observations and gave each other feedback. Initially, the 'guys' on the other lines watched with amusement and made wisecracks. Managers began making a point of congratulating the 'pilot' lines on how tidy the area was, and what a great thing they were doing for the company. After a few months, the other lines began to grumble about the attention the 'guinea pigs' were getting saying it was not fair and why couldn't they be involved. Management was pleased with others wanting to get involved, but was concerned incident rates were not dropping on the pilot lines.

At a food industry conference, they heard about another Behavioral Safety process that had reduced incidents by 54 percent in its first year. Their Behavioral Safety advisor, Pete, was invited to review the pilot process and make recommendations. He first asked to see the process design and implementation plan, but it did not exist. He then spoke to the 'guys' on the pilot lines asking for their comments. They said the process was 'OK' and it had helped with housekeeping, but little else. Too many people were observers and that affected production, as people took 'breaks' under the guise of observing. Others had to work faster just to keep up with production targets. They also said much more could be done with the data, but nobody knew what to do with them so the cards were put in the trash. Hazards had also been identified on the production line, but the supervisors kept telling them there wasn't any money in the budget to fix them. Worse, they felt like 'pariahs' as the other shifts kept giving them a hard time. Just to keep management happy, they did the observations, but thought it was all a pretty pointless exercise.

Pete reported back to management that the process lacked structure and the 'pilot' rollout had been divisive. He suggested they [1] develop an implementation plan that included everyone in the plant; [2] reduce the number of observers to one per shift, per line; [3] develop different checklists specific to the activities on the lines and other departments; [4] use the data to provide feedback and set improvement targets; and [5] provide sufficient resources in terms of a project team, and a budget to address any corrective actions. Within 12 months, under Pete's guidance, lost-time incidents reduced by 70 percent and minor incidents by 53 percent.

The effect of not having a clear process structure is clearly illustrated in Tabitha's pilot example where people were just going through the motions without any clear purpose. Isolating one group of people from other workers in pilot studies within the same business unit is also a mistake as it is divisive, creates unnecessary tensions, and can 'backfire' as people dismiss the process entirely. A good Behavioral Safety process will cover everyone's activities within a business unit from the outset.

Stamping structure on a Behavioral Safety process is the most important route to success. A lack of structure means the process is subject to the ebb and flows of the tides and usually ends up as 'driftwood'. Developing an implementation plan (see chapter 5) provides the necessary 'backbone' that allows for each element to be clearly defined with success factors built into each stage. Regardless of the approach adopted, the overall strategy broadly follows the same steps [1] assessment; [2] design; [3] implementation. The implementation rollout and execution stage should follow the project teams pre-developed implementation plan from the design stage. The sequence broadly follows [a] briefings; [b] project team training; [c] checklist development; [d] training; [e] observing; [f] using the observation data.

Usually by the time a Behavioral Safety process is ready to be rolled out, certain activities have already been completed. This would include [1] briefings; [2] project team recruitment and training; and [3] checklist development.

Briefings
If not already completed, briefings are designed to obtain 'buy-in'

from everyone in the various departments and 'shifts' (management and staff) at the very start. The idea is to inform people about the entire process, why it is designed the way it is, and what the process means to people individually and collectively. This helps ensure peoples support and involvement, and also provides an opportunity to seek and recruit project team members and observers.

The Process Champion should lead the briefing by explaining the site's previous incident history and why Behavioral Safety is seen as important to the company. Perhaps, it is due to a serious incident in recent times, or meeting corporate incident reduction targets, or both. Discussion of the issues should be encouraged. Although these can sometimes get 'lively', people's questions should be answered openly and honestly, so they do not leave the meeting feeling 'short-changed'. At the end of the meeting, it is also a good idea to ask people to identify safety problems and log and deal with them 'As Soon As is Practicable' (ASAP). The idea is to give the company the opportunity to demonstrate how serious it is about improving safety. Following up by publicizing what has been accomplished also creates 'goodwill' that helps to maintain 'buy-in' as the process is rolled-out.

Training Project teams

Project team members (see chapter 5) should have been trained in [1] selling the process to all; [2] designing the process; [2] checklist development; [3] observer training; [4] collating and analyzing observation data; [5] identifying barriers to sustainability. Simultaneously, the training period is used as a vehicle to help the team build their implementation plan. This training is generally conducted by professional advisors or in-house folks who have been 'trained as a trainer', and may require follow-up support coaching.

Checklist Development

If not done already data-mining techniques and other assessment methods should be used to identify those safety related behaviors implicated in the majority of incidents. The sequence for developing checklists (see chapter 7) is fairly straightforward: [1] identifying unsafe behaviors; [2] defining safe behaviors; [3] developing categories of behavior; [4] writing the behaviors [5] developing a recording format; and [6] reviewing and refining the checklists.

Safety behavior checklists should focus on very specific sets of behaviors, not contain categories of general behaviors that try to fix everything (e.g. Position = Line of fire, Falling, Pinch Points, Lifting). These are just too general to exert much (if any) impact on the behaviors of concern. For example, they are not tied to specific tasks and do not describe a single safe behavior that can be observed and interpreted in the same way by different observers.

Safety leadership checklists should focus on specific 'safety support' behaviors appropriate to the various levels of management that provide visible and demonstrable safety leadership. These safety leadership checklists should try to cover people, system, training, and process support behaviors.

Job-specific checklists should focus on the safety related behaviors that jobholders in administration and other support functions undertake in their job-role. For example, Human Resource personnel could focus on checking peoples training records to identify training needs, while Purchasing & Supply could focus on behaviors that ensure products are fit for purpose and safe to use.

The ultimate goal is to ensure behavioral checklists are targeting the safety related behaviors of everyone in the company, at each layer of the accident causation chain (see chapter 4). With everyone involved in observations of one form or another in their respective domains, the safety partnership will come to fruition and blossom, reducing incidents and their associated costs, while also contributing to increased efficiencies that lead to increased profits.

Rollout

When the background preparation work is complete, the true rollout begins. This often starts with observers being trained to use the checklists and provide coaching and feedback to those observed. This is usually followed up with a kick-off meeting and actual observations, data-analysis, and implementation of corrective actions.

Training

Due to the different Behavioral Safety process designs, there can be a variety of ways of approaching training. Key considerations surround who is to be trained, how many will be trained, and what type of training. The overall consideration is whether or not the training provides people with the right knowledge and skills to engage in the process. In most instances, this translates to 'the why', 'the what', 'the where', 'the when', and 'the how'.

Training Safety Observers

There is always more than one way of doing things. In some processes, particularly those using a 'one-on-one, peer-to-peer' approach, the idea is to *train everybody* to observe. Initially, this starts with people thought to be influential 'opinion formers', and then the training is rolled out to all, until such stage as a 'critical mass' has been achieved (usually 30-40 percent of the workforce). Depending on the number of people in a facility this can take 6-12 months or more, particularly as 'on-going' coaching of trained observers is required until all are comfortable and effective in their role. Some argue it is better to train everyone, even if they do not become observers, so that they are more familiar with the process and what it is trying to do. In this way they can decide to participate or not, on the basis of knowledge not speculation. In some implementations I have seen people vehemently against Behavioral Safety convert over the course of a day to become the most ardent and zealous advocates.

If a self-observation approach is adopted, everybody might require training in the development of a checklist, and possibly coaching and feedback skills (often these type of approaches widen their original scope to follow the traditional 'one-on-one, peer-to-peer' approach).

With the workgroup approach, a more measured pace to training is adopted with lower training requirements. Only one or two people per workgroup or shift are trained. These observers 'retire' after 4-6 months, and are replaced with the next wave of observers. Eventually everyone becomes an observer, but again depending on the number involved, this may take a few years. However, the effect is that everybody is observed pretty much from day one, unlike the 'one-on-one' approach, where the number of people being observed is highly dependent upon the number of trained observers available. I have heard from many workers in many different facilities that they have never been observed at all, even though the process has been going for some three years or more!

Training Managers

Every layer of management will require training in the use of their respective 'safety leadership' checklists and follow-up procedures (e.g. data-entry and corrective action follow-up). Generally, this takes about an hour. Additional training might (and should) also include teaching managers to conduct safety observations, and learning feedback and coaching skills.

Training Support Personnel

Support personnel (Human Resources, Purchasing & Supply, Engineering, Safety, Finance, etc.) training will be of the self-observation variety in the use of their respective 'Job Specific' checklists and the appropriate follow-up procedures.

Safety Observer Training Content

The content of safety observer training should cover all the basics, such as [1] why Behavioral Safety works; [2] what being an observer means; [3] where they will be observing; [4] when they should observe; and [5] how to [a] observe; [b] recognize resistance from others; [c] give verbal feedback and coach others. If a workgroup approach is adopted this would also include how to set improvement targets and run feedback meetings with their crews.

Some also teach observers to conduct either the '5-Why's' questioning technique, Hazard Identification, Risk Assessments, Job Safety Analyses (JSA's), or ABC analysis to enable observers to investigate the reasons for unsafe behaviors at the point of observation. The training should also involve 'field' observations so they can practice using their checklists under the guidance of the trainer. A close out meeting at the end of the day helps to clarify any queries.

Safety Leadership Training Content

There is an infinite variety of safety leadership courses ranging from those that are extremely comprehensive focusing on the 'why' of leadership to those that concentrate solely on the 'how' of leadership. Many of the comprehensive types attempt to cover the entire background to managerial leadership *per se,* focusing on personality, leadership style, and other 'self-examination' exercises, based on assumed links to organizational culture and leadership performance.

Others focus directly on what leaders should do in behavioral terms, such as communicating what they expect their personnel to do, observing their people on a day-to-day basis, and reinforcing good performance while discouraging bad performance. In my experience many managers prefer the latter approach, as it is firmly focused on the '*how*' of safety leadership, rather than the '*what*' and '*why*' which generally does not lead to concrete action.

Training Mediums

It is important that the trainee's interest is maintained throughout the training session. Often, classroom-training sessions are boring: either because of the content or the quality of training. The content and medium of delivery (e.g. solely documentation) might not be interesting and/or it is too packed, and people find it overwhelming. Equally the quality of the trainer will have a big influence. Many trainers have a monotonous voice that puts people to sleep, or 'lecture' at people rather than training them in the skills required. Sometimes, trainers do not really know the material, hoping to get by on 'a wing and a prayer'. Trainers must know their 'stuff'; otherwise the training is a wasted time and effort for all concerned. This is certainly one area where professional assistance should be considered, at least until 'internal' trainers become self-sufficient.

Whatever medium is used it must be well presented and organized, and follow a logical sequence where one activity builds on another. Think about the use of 'site made' video's and hands-on exercises and appropriate ways to involve people throughout the day. If an event is fun, people are more likely to remember the content for a long time after.

Training Schedules

Observer training is generally scheduled to last one day, though I have been in situations in construction and on some oil platforms where I have only had an hour! In these instances I have focused solely on how to use the checklist and observe, followed up with an hour's individual coaching at some point during the next day or two to teach feedback and coaching skills. In fact, it is a good idea to provide individual 'follow-on' coaching 'in the field' to reinforce the observer training for a short while (e.g. once a month per trained observer for 3- 6 months). This is known to increase their effectiveness three-fold.

Key Success Factors

Key success criteria would include [1] attendance [2] understanding of the process and supporting it; [2] being able to use the appropriate sampling tool; [3] being able to provide verbal feedback and coaching.

Kick-off Meetings

Project team members often hold Kick-off meetings once the observers are trained. In some facilities, these are equivalent to the briefings that should have been held at the very beginning of the process. Usually, this is because prior emphasis has been placed on selecting and training steering committee members, facilitators, and sponsor managers. This has then been followed up with managerial training, while the steering committee has concentrated on establishing itself and developing checklists. Often after 6 months or more of this preparation, the workforce is suddenly presented with a *fait accompli*. That is, the process is here, developed and ready to go; now you just have to do your part and be observed. Oh, and if you so desire you can become an observer too. In my view, this is why so many processes meet resistance from the workforce. They have not been involved until this point! The process is being done 'at' them, not 'with' them. This is the wrong way to establish a safety partnership.

To my mind these 'kick-off' meetings should be nothing more than a courtesy call to everyone, informing people that the process 'has gone live' and is being 'rolled-out'. These meetings should be thanking everyone for their help in developing the process, reminding them what happens from here on in, and asking for their continuing support. As such, the meetings should provide opportunities for questions, discussions, and clarifications. These meetings can also be accompanied with 'publicity'. For example, newsletters spelling out what the process is trying to achieve, how the process has been developed to date, and highlighting any corrective actions taken as a result of assessments, etc.

Observing Safety Behavior

The success of a Behavioral Safety process is entirely dependent on the regular sampling and recording of behavior. This formal data collection process is the key feature that distinguishes a Behavioral Safety process from other types of safety observation initiatives, such as weekly safety inspections or audits, and is one of the fundamental reasons they are so effective at reducing incident rates.

Behavioral observations are where a trained observer monitors his or her colleague's behavior in the workplace using a checklist of safety behaviors to record those behaviors observed. Based on Deming's principle that *'what gets measured gets done'* the observations increase the likelihood that people will behave safely. The data collected provides evidence about actual levels of safety behavior in a work area, facilitates the provision of feedback about performance, and induces ownership of safety by everyone. Thus observations are the 'bedrock' of the whole Behavioral Safety process.

Types of Observer

Many people are involved in conducting behavioral observations. These include project design members, senior managers, line-managers, supervisors, and employees in the different work areas. If contractors form part of the process, their personnel also observe their own people.

Senior Managers: Senior managers are not exempt from the observer's role. In fact their involvement is to be actively encouraged. The impact of senior management involvement in a UK metal refinery led to a 35 percent positive impact on the Percent Safe score, over an 18-month period. It's worth highlighting that *'management's reaction to change determines the success of change'*. Senior managers should demonstrate their safety leadership to all concerned to reinforce the point that the facility is taking the process seriously. To a large extent conducting observations also helps senior managers demonstrate they are personally fulfilling their statutory legislative duties. Even if senior managers do not conduct safety observations, they should still monitor and record their own 'supportive' safety leadership behaviors on a weekly basis (see chapter 7).

Line-Managers & Supervisors: It is important to involve line-managers and supervisors in the observer's role as this is known to increase the voluntary participation rates of employees in the observation process. They become more supportive of the process in general and much more familiar with the safety issues faced by hourly workers. Dealing with these provides further opportunities for them to demonstrate their safety leadership. Again, even if line-managers and supervisors do not conduct safety observations, they should still monitor and record their own 'safety leadership' behaviors on a weekly basis.

Employees: The vast majority of safety observers in a facility will be employees. To many, the involvement of the workforce in safety observations provides the stimulus for real change, as they tend to be the ones who are intimately familiar with the safety issues facing the workgroup. They are also the group of people who tend to be injured the most. Employee involvement also induces ownership of, and commitment to, safety *per se*, as probably for the first time in their working lives safety is being improved *'with'* them, instead of safety being done *'at'* them, as has traditionally been the case.

The total number of observers required should already be known from the design process (see chapter 5). The decisions simply reflect which type of observer (e.g. senior manager, employee) will observe whom, in which location.

Observation Frequency

The frequency of observation in a work area should also have been addressed at the planning and design stage. I would recommend daily observations as they have a much larger impact on the incident rate (see chapter 5). Although this is often decided by the observational approach adopted, it is very important that, regardless of approach, that work area observations are conducted at random so the timing of them is unpredictable. In general, the observers themselves actually decide when an observation will be conducted during their working day.

For a variety of reasons, observations are not always conducted. Within 'one-on-one, peer to peer', processes it is common for management or the project team to overcome this by setting observation quotas (Maturity level 2). For example, each person *will be observed*, or *will conduct* an observation once a month, or quarter. Often this leads to a massive number of observation cards being handed in at the end of the quota period, most of which focus on the use of PPE or unsafe conditions. This should raise suspicions about their authenticity. It also indicates the process has merely become a numbers game. In my view it is much better to target the quality of observations, as they are more likely to reduce the incident rate. Quantity by itself will not guarantee this, particularly with general 'catch-all' observation cards type processes. If your company has adopted 'quantity' as its primary measure of success, the number of cards 'turned-in' should be correlated with incident rates over a 12-month period. This should help to determine if the approach is useful or not. If incident rates have stayed the same or worsened, the quota system should be abolished, and the emphasis switched to quality of observations.

Most workgroup approaches try to achieve one daily observation per workgroup, though some also use 2-3 times per week. By and large the number of observations is usually achieved without too much effort. In some processes I have helped implement, other workgroup members have become very enthusiastic and also want to observe every day. This has resulted in the coordinator catering for this administratively, so as not to disappoint.

Observation Strategy

Treating people with the same respect they would desire for themselves, good observers are open and honest. A person is observed against the behaviors on the observation checklists. Those performed safely are recorded as such, those unsafely are recorded and discussed at the end of the observation, with feedback and /or coaching provided.

Without checklists to use as a guide, observing people's behavior in the workplace is often not as easy as it sounds. Sometimes a small difference in a behavior cannot be readily observed, or the behavior is conducted with such speed that it is difficult to see. This means that observers need to learn to focus on what people are *actually* doing, not on what they *think* people might be doing. In such instances talking to the person doing the job can clarify these issues.

Also because people become used to seeing others behave unsafely (i.e. people have always done it that way) they are often 'blind' to how unsafe some behaviors really are. Standing back and asking 'How might someone get injured here' can overcome this. For example, the position of someone's hand when holding the 'spur' on a forklift truck steering wheel could result in a thumb being broken or bruised. If the person's hand is in an 'upright' fist, with the thumb placed on top and the vehicle wheels hit an obstacle on the floor, the 'spur' will automatically be caught safely or be freed when it 'kicks'. If the fist is on the horizontal plane, and the wheel kicks, a thumb slightly out of place could be bruised or broken. This is one of the reasons that checklists focused on 'specific' behaviors are so much better at impacting the incident rate: they tell the observer exactly what to look for.

Different strategies may be useful for enhancing the effectiveness of the process. It is certainly a good idea to observe when dangerous or hazardous activities are being performed, or other 'abnormal' circumstances apply (e.g. during machine downtime), as this is the time people are most likely to get hurt. Some ask observers from one department or location to observe others in different locations. On the surface this has some merit, as a fresh pair of eyes sees things others don't. In my experience, however, people prefer accepting feedback from people they know, not a 'stranger'. That's not to say that you should not intervene if you see someone in imminent danger of being hurt!

A few innovative ideas (not mine) suggest using a mix of observation strategies. One is to allow or encourage additional observations from 'non-observers'. This means everyone in the facility carries 'blank' observation cards with them in their 'back-pocket', which they use 'as and when' it's appropriate. A slightly different approach is to allow people to create their own focused checklists, and monitor themselves, in addition to the 'official' observations. These two approaches offer the advantage of 24/7 observations being done in an area, when the 'official' observers have yet to do theirs, or have already done them. Another innovative twist is to put control of being observed into the hands of people who want to be observed. This refers to a person asking to be observed by someone else: an 'official' observer, a project team member, a supervisor or a colleague, to help ensure they are working safely. These ideas have considerable merit as they are all directed at people taking personal responsibility for their own actions and they overcome some of the problems often encountered when Behavioral Safety is done 'at' people, not 'with' them.

Observation Challenges

A number of known observation challenges include:

Observers don't know the behaviors on their observation checklist. Although this improves with practice, the data collected during the initial stages is not as accurate as it could be, simply because observers spend time looking for an item on the checklist. This means they often miss other unsafe behaviors being performed. It is a good idea to introduce a one or two-week practice period, where the data collected is used solely to make sure all observers are recording accurately. Interestingly, safety behavior tends to improve during this practice period

Observers don't behave safely themselves. An observer who does not behave safely will soon lose credibility with his or her peers. This means an observer *must set a good example all of the time, he or she is at work.* I recall hearing the phrase 'steam curtain' on a plant. I asked what this was and one of the guys said they would show me. As we went through the control room, fully kitted out with PPE, one of the supervisors stopped me to ask a question. This conversation took longer than expected, and at some point I had taken my protective glasses off and put them in my pocket. The guy who was showing me the 'steam curtain' came back and asked me to hurry up as he had others things to do. I rushed out after him, and forgot to put my glasses back on. As soon as I stepped on the plant, five workers pulled me up! All that day I took a lot of 'ribbing' from everyone on the plant, everywhere I went. An unpleasant experience caused by my own stupidity. The positive was that at least the guys did pull me up (they had been resistant to the process to begin with).

Observed practices appear so trivial they do not seem important. It is usually the seemingly trivial things that trigger an incident. For example, a stone in a walkway and someone not looking where they are going could lead to a turned ankle. Similarly, a signaler for crane operations could be in the wrong position to maintain eye contact with the crane operator, and the swinging load could crush someone.

Signalers should always maintain a clear line of sight with the crane operator (even when using radios). In some facilities, I have seen the signalers view of the crane operator blocked by equipment and machinery during a 'lift', when all the signaler had to do was position themselves in such a way, that they could maintain eye contact throughout the entire operation. My grandmother taught me from a very young age *'look after the pennies and the pounds will take care of themselves'.* This same principle applies to safety behavior: Look after the 'seemingly' trivial issues and the big problems just don't arise!

The observers never have the time to actually observe. Many people are very busy at work, and often are so busy, that they do not feel that they can take the time from their production duties to observe. In some cases people just do not observe because they do not want to. Tracking the frequency of missed observations against expectations is a useful indicator that can signal difficulties for a particular observer to facilitate problem solving.

Minimizing the observation time often helps. Many processes ask observers to spend a few minutes observing one person and giving feedback and any necessary coaching. Those using workgroup observations generally take between 10-15 minutes, for one person, per day. Managerial observations can often be done as part of manager's normal duties, taking just a few minutes to have a safety conversation with someone.

Colleagues do not like being observed. Sometimes, people become upset when they are observed. Usually this occurs when a facility adopts a 'peer-to-peer' observational approach, and people's 'buy-in' or assistance was not sought at the very beginning of the process. Often, this is due to 'resentment' arising from the process being done 'at' people, not with them.

Of course, there are always the ten percent of those who will always be vehemently 'anti' for philosophical or other reasons. Do not get into an argument with them. It is usually a complete waste of time, as they just end up becoming more fixed in their views. I once took this tack with a guy in a chemical factory, who had begun to berate me for introducing the process into the factory. I 'bit my tongue' and walked away saying I would talk to him at another time when he was calmer. Two weeks later he asked how he could help out. I looked at him and immediately said 'Who got hurt'? One of his colleagues had slipped into a hot acid bath and 'cooked' his foot, and would be off work for 6 months or more! Unfortunately, it is often the way. Someone has to pay the price and get hurt before the 'anti's' realize the process is for their benefit (if implemented properly).

Verbal Feedback

To be effective, feedback *has* to be specific, relevant, credible, frequent, timely, and linked to action sources. Most, if not all, Behavioral Safety processes train and encourage people to give verbal feedback at the point of observation: either to provide positive feedback to reinforce safe behavior, or coach the person to behave safely.

For many this takes courage, particularly if the observed is someone unknown (e.g. contractor, visitor). It also requires respect for others, tact, skill, and an understanding of the issues. Charging in like a 'bull in a china shop' puts people on the defensive, which makes them less receptive to listening to the message. If you remember the quotation *'a communication not received is not a communication at all'* to guide your efforts you will not go too far wrong.

Good feedback is designed to be of value to the receiver, not an emotional release for the supplier. The key to verbal feedback is to make people feel relaxed and at ease. This means the 'supplier' has to be careful of their body language and tone of voice. People do not just hear what is said, they are also conscious of the way it is said. It's difficult to bring the 'barriers' down once they have gone up!

It is much easier for those giving feedback to focus on the specific behavior in question, based on facts not inferences of what they 'thought' they saw. In other words relevant and credible. Feedback also has to be frequent. This is one of the reasons why observation 'contact rates' need to be regular. If an observation is only done once a month or more, feedback to a person or group of people is not going to be frequent, and therefore will be much less effective. It is the constant, timely 'drip, drip' of attention that changes people's behavior, not an occasional 'big bang'.

A good observer stops to *listen to the answers* before responding. On one site during a coaching session a guy had been observed pulling up some materials with a rope, without wearing a hardhat. We were on the ground and climbed 7 flights of stairs to speak to the guy. He was asked what he thought he had done unsafely. He started to speak and mentioned 3 or four unsafe acts that we had not been able to observe from the ground, but the observer enthusiastically cut him off and proceeded to talk about the hard hat. After we had walked away, I coached the observer about how important listening skills were and pointed out how many other unsafe behaviors the guy was telling us about. He took the point, and became remarkably adept at listening and resolving problems.

At all times, an observer should be prepared to help the recipient find ways of resolving problem issues that may be holding them back from behaving safely. At one construction site that was way behind schedule, an experienced welder was wearing all the required PPE, but his young helper was only wearing light eye protection while holding a metal bracket in place. When the issue was discussed and feedback given, it was found the welder believed clear polycarbonate safety glasses would protect the helper against 'welders eye' (It's a lot like getting a sunburn, only it's in your eye) because they were coated with anti-UV material, and the helper was not looking directly at the 'flash'. It was pointed out these were good if the guy was 15 feet away. He was asked to wait a couple of minutes while appropriate eye protection was arranged to be brought down to the site. A quick radio call to the stores and 'hey presto', job done. Had the observer not tried to help out, and walked away after giving feedback, his credibility would have been shot to pieces! Although the welder was a bit upset with us for 'holding up the job', the young guy thanked the observer later for helping him out. He was uncomfortable with what he was doing, but did not want to create a scene with the older guy, who was 'quick-tempered'.

This illustrates that with many observers in the workplace, small-scale equipment and resource issues *are* going to arise. The company must be prepared to resolve these quickly and efficiently. Corrective action resolution is a different form of feedback, but most vital.

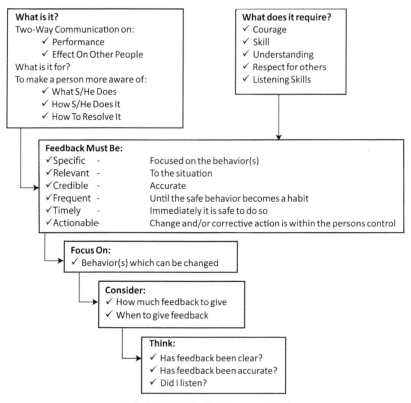

Exhibit 8.1: Verbal Feedback Tips

Summary

Rollout requires careful planning and perfect execution as this is the point where everything starts to come together, and is everyone's 'first taste' of the process in action. If it goes badly, it will affect everything that follows. Structuring the process to provide a 'backbone' helps to ensure all goes smoothly and helps to maintain the integrity of the process. Many potential 'pitfalls' should be avoided if you have carefully thought through the issues during the implementation planning and have adhered to the plan. However, do be flexible and adapt to changing situations as they arise. After rollout, the most difficult trick is to maintain and sustain the process.

9 Maintain To Sustain

With great fanfare, Behavioral Safety briefings and Cultural Web exercises had been conducted with the entire workforce, generating a list of over 300 corrective actions. Checklists had been developed for all plant areas. Seventy percent of the workforce had volunteered and been trained in observation and feedback skills. Managers at all levels had developed 'Safety Leadership' checklists and monitored themselves against those each week. The shift crews had set their own improvement targets and discussed the results of the observations at the beginning of each shift cycle. A site summary of all results was presented to the senior management team every week. With incident rates consistently heading 'south' for the previous nine months, senior management was very pleased with the process.

Palmer, a divisional safety manager was appointed to the site as the manufacturing manager as part of his career progression having just completed an MBA. Involved on the fringes of the Behavioral Safety process in the factory in his previous role, Palmer decided that a feedback meeting every week for each shift was too much. The project team highlighted the potential adverse impact on safety performance. Palmer did not think it would matter, so long as one feedback meeting was held monthly, and besides it would increase productivity. Over the next four weeks, 25 minor injuries occurred. The project team successfully argued for the feedback meetings to be restored. Incident rates began to reduce, but after two months they were still at pre-implementation levels.

A pre-planned annual review of the process was held. This revealed a dramatic drop-off in employee participation and observation rates. The project team spoke with everyone to discover the reasons. They were told supervisors said production was now the number one priority. Supervisors were discouraging people from observing more than once per shift cycle. Weekly feedback meetings were now only a 5-minute presentation of results, instead of the 30-minute discussion meetings that happened before they were stopped. Some of the guys had complained to Palmer, who had then stopped them working overtime, giving it to others who were more compliant. Corrective actions were also being 'put on hold' as the budget had been slashed. The workforce were simply withdrawing from the process.

Despondent, the project team presented their findings to the management team and asked for the full support they had previously enjoyed. The project team pleaded with Palmer to at least try and walk in the previous manager's shoes, especially with his safety background. Palmer said the economic climate was forcing his hand and people would just have to get used to the new regime. Over the next 12-months fewer and fewer observation sheets were being turned in. With incident rates showing no improvement, the project team meetings also began to stop. Nobody seemed to take notice. Eventually the entire process came to a grinding halt.

The above example shows how a well designed and executed Behavioral Safety process can be turned into a train wreck! *The major underlying reason that 99 percent of all Behavioral Safety processes fail is a loss of credibility.* This usually means the process is not 'living up to its promises' in some way. The question is how to avoid getting to this stage. The answer is to build in a wide range of *systemic checks and balances.* For example, [1] collating and analyzing data; [2] placing graphical feedback charts in the working areas so people can see the trends in their performance; [3] setting improvement targets; [4] holding regular workforce feedback meetings to facilitate discussion of the observations and identify corrective actions; [5] monitoring the completion of corrective actions; [6] monitoring process 'scorecards'; [7] creating dedicated 'focus groups' who look at particular topic issues; [8] conducting in-depth data analysis to highlight the peaks and troughs in data trends; [9] cross-checking the behaviors involved in incidents against those on observation checklists; and [10] conducting regular performance reviews of the entire process and the performance of the project team. Together these help to maintain real involvement and transparency, which in turn helps sustainability.

Collating and Analyzing Data

Collating and analyzing data is one of the fundamental elements of a good Behavioral Safety process as this allows *safety* strengths and weaknesses to be identified in a multitude of areas. It also allows Key Performance Indicators (KPI's) to be used to monitor the effectiveness of the *process.*

Safety strengths and weaknesses are identified by 'drilling' into the observation data itself to highlight issues associated with management, methods, materials, manpower, and machinery. Common Behavioral Safety *process* KPI's include [a] participation rates; [b] observation rates; [c] percent safe scores; [d] safety leadership scores; [e] corrective action rates; [f] the number of feedback meetings held; [g] visible ongoing support rates; [h] number of near-hits reported; [i] amount of positive praise given; [j] amount of constructive feedback given; and [k] quality of observations.

Key Performance Indicators

Participation rates are used mostly in 'one-on-one, peer-to-peer' processes as they are highly dependent upon the number of people who have been trained and who are actively taking part. These can be calculated for wage-roll employees, different managerial levels, and those completing self-observations in the support functions (e.g. Human Resources).

Observation rates refer to the number of observations actually being completed, compared to those expected, and is a common KPI used in all forms of Behavioral Safety processes.

The *'Percent Safe'* score is also used in most Behavioral Safety processes. Essentially reflecting the ratio of safe to unsafe behaviors this KPI is used to provide an indicator of the levels of safe behaviors being performed and is often trended over time. Regular troughs are examined to identify the reasons (which can be many and varied, including events outside of the workplace). It is also used to facilitate workgroup goal setting. Initial observations are used as a baseline for comparative purposes. Subsequently, improvement targets are set by each workgroup or area, and the data is then tracked through to goal-achievement.

Safety leadership scores for different levels of management, reflect the ratio between enacted and non-enacted safety leadership behaviors (generally recorded at weekly intervals). These provide an indication of the levels of managerial support being provided, and are usually separated by senior, middle, and front-line management levels.

The corrective action rate refers to the number of corrective actions completed, compared to the total number reported in a given time period (usually within 30 days)

The number of feedback meetings held is used mostly in workgroup based Behavioral Safety approaches, but provides an indicator that time is being set aside for work crews to discuss the results of their safety observations and decide upon appropriate corrective actions.

Visible Ongoing Support rates refer to observers indicating enacted or non-enacted support behaviors they are aware of from managers, project team members, and their colleagues. This is often used to provide a crosscheck on the levels of safety leadership indicated by management, and highlights areas where project team members can provide more support to work crews.

The number of near-hits reported is a useful KPI of how seriously the Behavioral Safety process is being taken by everybody. Often, the frequency of reporting increases as people realize the data will be used in a meaningful way by the project teams and others to get things done to ensure similar circumstances do not arise. Often, the reporting of minor injuries previously hidden also increases as the process takes hold, and people become less fearful they will be 'shot' for bringing 'bad news' to people's attention. Although there can be an initial surge in reporting minor incidents (e.g. scratches), which appears to make the process look weak, after about 6-9 months the numbers tend to fall as the process takes effect.

The *quality of observations* are assessed by comparing Percent Safe scores for particular checklists behaviors against those identified on near-hit reports and incident records. As the Percent Safe scores that are recorded increase (e.g. for wearing gloves) the associated injuries should decrease (e.g. hand injuries).

Some processes also use the *amount of positive praise given* as a KPI. Usually, these are the processes that place a heavy emphasis on 'consequence' management. Some monitor the ratio of positive feedback given to the number of times people have been coached for unsafe behavior. This positive to negative ratio should be about 4:1. An increasing number of *'positive praises'* should also be reflected in corresponding reductions in incidents. If the number of praises increases and incident rates stay the same, there is something amiss. It would be worth examining if the praise given is being directed at incident causing behaviors.

The amount of constructive feedback given refers to the use of feedback and coaching in the 'field' at the point of observation, and is often recorded on observation cards in 'one-on-one' approaches. This provides an indicator of the number of times observers are giving verbal feedback and coaching. This data is often compared to other KPI's such as observation rates.

Collectively, these KPI's provide a comprehensive overview of the effectiveness of the process. As achievement levels on these KPI's increase there should also be proportional reductions in incident frequency and severity rates. If there is not, something is not right and a comprehensive process review should immediately be undertaken. This should be conducted by someone with in-depth knowledge of Behavioral Safety, but independent of the facilities project team.

Although the Safety Leadership and Corrective Action rates are the most difficult KPI's to achieve they exert the most fundamental influence on safety performance. The Safety Leadership scores demonstrate that managers *are* leading for safety, while the Corrective Action rate is feedback to the workforce that the company is taking the process very seriously. In combination with the other KPI's (e.g. Percent Safe) these provide 'proof positive' the company is traveling on the safety partnership journey.

Graphical Feedback Charts

Posting visual performance data on large graphical feedback charts provides knowledge of progress toward goal-achievement (often implicitly 100% safe), which can be motivating. If people do not know how well they are doing, they certainly cannot adjust their performance to improve. The graphs need to be designed so they can be readily understood by anyone at a glance. As shown in Exhibit 9.1, the vertical axis usually presents Percent Safe, with the horizontal axis representing time.

In some processes, these types of chart are computer generated. The main point is they should be on display, to provide an overview of progress. Ideally, these should be placed so people can see the trends in their own areas performance. Plant or site wide charts could also be placed at the main site entrance.

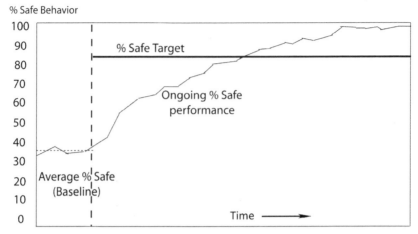

Exhibit 9.1: Example Graphical Feedback Chart

Improvement Targets

Although feedback on its own can change behavior and reduce injuries, it is much more effective when coupled with safety targets. This is because targets are motivational as they focus people's attention on the actions required to achieve it. Behavioral Safety evidence shows targets jointly set by people are far superior to those assigned by others (e.g. steering committees, supervisors, etc) at reducing incident rates. The likely reason is that as people jointly work out the best ways to achieve something, they also tend to be more committed to achieving that something.

Average levels of behavioral performance observed at the beginning of a process are used as the starting point to help people set their own targets. The average Percent Safe score for the first week or so is used as a comparison point in the future and is termed the 'baseline period'. In essence the baseline period reflects the levels of measured safety behavior prior to the process 'biting and taking effect'.

The safety behavior targets should be SMART: **S**pecific (e.g. a 25 percent improvement in safety behavior); as **M**easured with the observation checklists; **A**greed with those who have to achieve them; **R**ealistic (not too easy, not too hard); and **T**ime bound (within a pre-determined period of time). In some processes, targets are changed as soon as the original target has been reached. In others, the target is set for a specific period of time to allow certain safety behaviors to become habitual. Although usually reserved for the Percent Safe scores, targets could also be set for Safety Leadership scores, and Visible Ongoing Support Scores.

In terms of the *process* KPI's, it is useful to aim to achieve a 95 percent compliance target. For example, 95 percent of the Corrective actions will be completed every month. Other process KPI's lending themselves to this include Participation and Observation Rates (wage-roll employees and managers); Constructive feedback (i.e. 95 percent of observers give constructive feedback, 95 percent of the time); and Quality of Observations (e.g. 95 percent of the behaviors involved in near-hits and incidents after the process is in effect for a month or two, are *not* on the observation checklists).

SUMMARY OF BEHAVIORAL CATEGORIES

Sub-heading Number	Category	No. of SAFES	No. of UNSAFES	No. of NOT SEEN	% SAFE Performances	% of Observations
01	Equipment	122	32	20	79.2	37.45
02	Stairs	56	12	5	82.4	16.55
03	Shelves	80	2	0	97.6	19.95
04	Laboratory	63	44	4	58.9	26.05
etc.						
Grand Totals		321	90	29	78.1	100

Three Best Scoring Items

Item No.	Heading	Checklist Item Text	Number of Safes Recorded
16	Laboratory	Jars are labeled correctly	45
2	Equipment	Tools are stored away after use	37
8	Stairs	People are holding the handrail	26

Three Worst Scoring Behaviors

Item No.	Heading	Checklist Item Text	Number of Safes Recorded
17	Laboratory	Spills & Leaks not cleaned	27
5	Equipment	Obstructing emergency doors/ equipment	20
9	Stairs	Stairs are free of obstruction	12

Exhibit 9.2: Example Tabulated Feedback Report

Weekly Feedback Meetings

Holding regular workforce feedback meetings helps to facilitate discussion of the observation data to identify corrective actions, which in turn helps people achieve their improvement targets. To achieve this, the observation data for a work area or work team needs to be collated and analyzed to produce a tabulated report that highlights both strengths and weaknesses. The strengths provide opportunities for praise, while the weaknesses highlight areas that should be targeted for problem solving.

The target - weekly feedback - corrective action cycle is shown in Exhibit 9.3. Once an improvement target is set, the following week the shift team, work area employees, etc., receive the written, tabulated feedback report that is particular to their behavioral performance. After discussion of the results, the crew decides upon an action focus (usually the top three worst scoring behaviors). Discussions would focus on why those particular behaviors are a problem and what corrective actions are required. In this way, by a process of attrition, problems are resolved whether condition or behavior based, or both. The following week, the tabulated feedback report would indicate whether the issues have been resolved. If they have, the crew moves onto the next area presenting opportunities for improvement, and so on.

Exhibit 9.3: Target and Feedback Cycle

Corrective Actions

Monitoring the completion of corrective actions arising from the Behavioral Safety process is the most effective method for keeping people involved. This is because they can see that the unsafe conditions and other issues are being addressed, which transmits the message to all concerned that the process is being taken seriously. This prompts them to look for other issues that need resolving, until eventually they run out of things to report. This can be clearly seen in

Exhibit 9.4, where initially some 385 jobs were raised in the first 6 months (Phase 1) in a refinery, which diminished to 48 new jobs by the end of phase 3, some 18 months later. The jobs ranged in scope from painting yellow lines on the edges of steps to highlight their potential as a tripping hazard, to building an extension on the 'mess hall' so people could put their hard hats and coats on hooks while eating.

Phase	Jobs Raised	Completed Jobs	% Complete
1	385	294	76%
2	167	206	123%
3	48	61	127%
Total	600	561	93.5%

Exhibit 9.4: Corrective Actions Completed every Six Months

This data can be further broken down into departments or job functions as shown in Exhibit 9.5, which immediately highlights where corrective actions are being addressed in the company. The irony in this example is the safety department was the laggard!

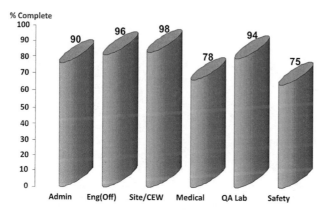

Exhibit 9.5: Corrective Action Rate by Department

If there is not one already, a corrective action system will need to be developed. This usually comprises of a 'corrective action planning process' (once an issue is reported), an 'implementation schedule' (which should be set at a maximum of 30 days for issues not requiring capital expenditure) and an 'evaluation process' that ensures the action has made matters better, not created other problems. Many companies will assign a 'notional' budget to their Behavioral Safety process for corrective actions. Usually this is in the form of a 'cost code' that can be used to track expenditure.

Managerial Scorecards

Giving regular, relevant, and timely feedback is important to keep Senior Management fully engaged in the process. The feedback should provide a 'helicopter' view of the entire process across the whole site: This usually means collating and providing a summary of the data for every Behavioral Safety KPI being used. These are presented at senior site management meetings, usually by a member of the project team. Some sites prefer to receive this information every week, others every month. In my experience, the senior management team asks searching questions and prompts appropriate actions, which they expect to be resolved by the next meeting. This is the true value of presenting the data. Senior management keeps their finger on the pulse of the project, which keeps them engaged. It also helps to keep the process on schedule and helps to ensure sustainability.

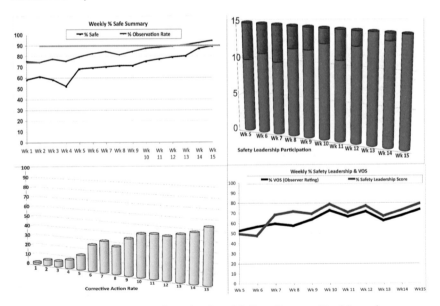

Exhibit 9.6: Example Behavioral Safety Process Dashboard

Presentations to senior management teams should also include a SWOT assessment (i.e. Strengths, Weaknesses, Opportunities, and Threats). Completing this weekly helps the project team stay on track, while also informing senior management of positive aspects and potential obstacles.

STRENGTHS	WEAKNESSES
1. 1st Weekly B-Safe® Newsletter released 2. Managers / Shift Supervisors being trained as observers 3. Shipping Dept. feedback meetings begin 4. Roll-out proceeding according to schedule in finance Dept. 5. Corrective Actions being addressed 6. Safest workgroup of the week campaign being announced / proceeding	1. Not all observers observing consistently 2. Not all observers 'turning in' completed checklists daily 3. EMS not doing any observations - re-training required 4. Not all managers recording Safety Leadership support
OPPORTUNITIES	THREATS
1. Weak observers being identified & retrained	1. Some Project Team members being denied access to internal IT systems, because no password. Delaying in-depth data analysis.

Exhibit 9.7: Example SWOT Assessment

Topic Focus Groups

Another way of keeping people interested and motivated is to create dedicated 'Topic Focus Groups' who look at particularly important issues highlighted in the observation data. These could be set up by the project team or other teams (e.g. quality) to create synergy between the two. This is a good way of linking the Behavioral Safety process into the company's mainstream management systems. Restricted entirely by your own imagination, dedicated Focus Groups found alongside Behavioral Safety processes include [1] Near-hit and Incident Investigation; [2] Process Safety; [3] Ergonomics; [4] Industrial Hygiene; [5] Safety Training; [6] Environmental; and [7] Publicity/Celebrations/Marketing.

A Focus Group typically comprises of 7-10 individuals drawn from various site locations and job functions, usually selected or appointed because they have some knowledge of a particular topic and can make a valuable contribution. The issues they discuss are generated from an analysis of the Behavioral Safety process data, which has highlighted the topics particular importance. The purpose is to arrive at cost-effective and realistic solutions. For example, plant employees reported a problem accessing valves that were just out of reach from the floor. They had to stand on ladders to use their 'Wheel-dogs' to turn the valves. This required someone to hold the ladder, while another shift technician turned the valve. This was not easy, as it was difficult to exert the required pressure on 'sticky' valves while standing on a ladder. A Process Safety Focus Group examined the site location, and talked with designers to cost potential solutions. The choices were installing cat ladders to a platform or lowering the valves. One of the operators had suggested small concrete plinths with three risers with sufficient depth to safely stand on. This proved to be the simplest and cheapest option. These provided a solid base, with sufficient room for the technicians to place their body to exert the maximum amount of pressure. The solution also reduced the manpower requirement for the task to a 'one-man job'. Other actions included developing an observation checklist to include Process Safety issues such as pipe work lagging, short studs, redundant scaffolding, Steam Tracing/ Trap Leaks, etc. The advantages of topic Focus Groups, therefore, are that particular problems are examined; group members influence each other by responding to each other's ideas and comments; and, innovative and cost-effective solutions are provided.

In-depth Data Analysis

The sheer number of observations recorded in a well-designed Behavioral Safety process provides a rich tapestry of behavior patterns across a facility. If these are collated in software and analyzed it is possible to identify the multitude of influences affecting safe and unsafe behavior. These influences will include the behavior of managerial and technical systems, machinery, task processes, *and* societal factors. For example, in a Cellophane plant we identified the influence of workers 'community service' on the Percent Safe score and poor maintenance planning on incident rates. The sites average Percent Safe score dropped by 6 percentage points, with 25 minor incidents over 4 weeks, compared to 4 in the previous four-week period. The community service caused significant amounts of fatigue as workers built 'floats' for the towns annual festival after their 'shifts' finished, which in turn reduced the Percent Safe score. In combination with poor maintenance planning where all jobs were scheduled to occur in the same area at the same time, not in a sequence, the number of minor injuries rose. This illustrates there may be more than one factor influencing behavior and injury rates. However, we only discovered what these were by examining the reasons for the drop off in safety performance data. Thus, the peaks and troughs in the data trends are important indicators of potential problems.

Significant, sustained troughs in the trends signal the need to look underwater at the base of the iceberg (see chapter 4). The starting place is to examine which specific behaviors are causing the drop. This provides clues about whether the problem is related to physical task issues, managerial issues, or observation issues. Physical task issues may be related to changes in equipment, processes and procedures. Managerial issues could be related to productivity pushes, decreases in manpower levels, lack of crew feedback meetings, or corrective actions not being addressed. Observation issues could include inaccurate observations, the number of observations that are below expectations, etc. Comparing trends of all relevant Key Performance Indicators could help to affirm or refute potential reasons, ultimately leading to the right solutions.

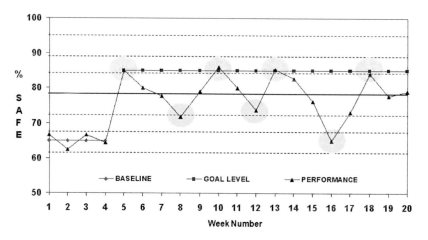

Exhibit 9.8: Percent Safe Peaks and Troughs

In Exhibit 9.8 a workgroups Percent Safe scores consistently worsened every four weeks, and climbed back to target within a week or two. Initially, this had been treated as normal variation, but after the third month an examination of the root causes was undertaken. It was found that Permit to Work issuers rotated every two weeks, and the one on duty when performance slumped, had a habit of keeping personnel waiting for a couple of hours while he ensured the paperwork was 'just so', and then issued almost twice as many as the other person, but still expected the jobs to be completed within the same day. This increased time pressure caused people to rush and take short-cuts. This finding led to a task force being set up to overhaul the entire Permit-to-Work system. The example illustrates the sensitivity of the Percent Safe data when quality observations are undertaken and how it can assist to identify problems in other areas of activity that are affecting safety behavior.

Quality of Observations

An objective method for determining the quality of observations is to cross-check the behaviors involved in near-hits and injury causing incidents against those on observation checklists, *as soon as possible after these are reported*. If any are found, examine the Percent Safe score for that behavior or category over a time period. Has that behavior been fluctuating? Has there been a consistent improvement? Has it consistently got worse? If the behavior has consistently been recorded as safe, but is involved in more than a couple of incidents there is a problem: Either in interpretation of the behavior or the timing of observations. If there is a problem in interpretation, clarify the wording on the checklist to remove ambiguity. To address issues related to the timing of observations, examine the incident records for the time of incidents and day of the week to see if there is a pattern emerging. If so, encourage observers to observe that behavior at that time, on the day(s) identified, in the location where the incident occurred.

Doing this also helps the project team identify and keep track of unsafe behaviors that are involved in current incidents. These can be bought to people's attention and placed on revised checklists when appropriate.

Publicity and Celebrations

Publicity and celebrations are primarily concerned with the *'Marketing'* of the process. Often the marketing effort is introduced at the initial phases with a great deal of noise and then fades away over time. It is very important to keep it going, though it may need to be reinvented or adapted as time goes by. *Creativity is the key*. Think of ways you can integrate and use your process name, logo, slogans and results to fire people's imagination. Be edgy and push boundaries. You want people to eagerly await the next publication or event, in the same way as the adverts for the 'Super Bowl' are eagerly anticipated each year. You want people to talk about it amongst themselves once the material is published or released. Most good campaigns have various phases: a *Tease phase* that prepares the ground (e.g. our Behavioral Safety process is coming and the benefits are ....); an *Excite phase* suggesting exciting things are going to happen and what the benefits will be (e.g. Our Behavioral Safety process will deliver....!); an *Involve phase* that gets people involved in the process (e.g. become part of the process and benefit by......); and a *Sustain phase* that helps keep the momentum of the process going (e.g. we are achieving ....!, this benefits us by ......!). The hallmarks of a great marketing campaign are continuity, distinctiveness, courage, and fun. Together these should convey the company's passion for the process.

Tease Phase: The initial briefings to everyone about the process are the 'tell and sell' stage, and nobody will 'buy-in' if there are no direct benefits to them. Think about the 'Unique Selling Points' of the Behavioral Safety process compared to other safety efforts, and how best to target the message to the audience. For example, selling the idea of a genuine 'safety partnership' is quite novel in some companies and industries and it gets people excited about the possibilities.

Excite Phase: Having prepared the ground with the site assessment, think of ways to promote the findings, the different ways that issues are to be addressed and how this will provide benefits to people and the company. Reinforce the message to let people know this is a serious effort. For example, managers could ask 'what can I do to improve your safety?' and then follow through with the appropriate actions.

Involve Phase: This phase usually takes place once the training of project team members has begun and checklists are being developed. The marketing campaign should focus on what is happening, and how people can become involved as observers, or help to develop checklists, etc. In one facility we asked the workforce for help to go through the sites records of the previous three-year accident history to identify specific unsafe behaviors. On average, twenty volunteers would show after their shift or on their days off to help out. These guys then helped to recruit observers. In other words, they believed in the process and what it promised on the basis of our marketing efforts. This stage should also be used to get the workforce to develop a name, slogan, and logo for the process through competitions, or to submit 'copy' for publication.

Process launch or 'kick-off' events should be exciting and 'news-worthy' but also extremely well organized and 'on message'. For example, we have launched the 'going live' stage by taking observers to the local sport team's next home match (which happened to be a soccer semi-final), where a 'meal and speeches' took place, followed by everyone watching the match. This event is still talked about 10 years later! In others we have used employee giveaways (information leaflets, mugs, tee-shirts, baseball caps, key chains, pens, etc) to reinforce the message.

Sustain Phase: Once the process has started, the sustain phase kicks in. This stage is often the one that isn't maintained, but is probably the most important. Make use of the old adage *'success breeds success'* to publicize and celebrate all the successes spinning out of the process. These should provide much of the material for a sustained marketing campaign (If you are not achieving any, then something is wrong with process!).

It is important that the company awards and celebrations are geared toward workgroups, not individuals! This approach explicitly recognizes that 'safety' is a group activity, where everyone is dependent upon everyone else working safely. In Nigeria on a construction project with 20,000 workers, we awarded a B-Safe® 'flag' to the 'safest workgroup' of the week. Initially, each workgroups Percent Safe scores were compared. Project team members independently assessed the top three scoring workgroups. If just one unsafe behavior was observed during the assessment, the workgroup was discounted for the award that week. People went to extraordinary lengths improving their safety to 'win' the award and keep it. We also did the same for the most improved workgroup. The workgroups would appear in the weekly 'safety newsletter' which was distributed to all on the site. The reason it worked so well was because people were 'proud' of belonging to the site's safest workgroup, which gave them 'elite' status. In other words, the idea is to use 'social recognition' on a grand scale. Be clear about the objective criteria required to 'win' an award, and make sure the process is as transparent as possible.

There are many other forms of publicity that can be used to help maintain and sustain the Behavioral Safety process. These include regular internal newsletters that keep people informed about progress and particular actions. These often include pictures of personnel who have been outstanding in some way, and 'before and after' corrective actions, and reports of celebration events. Some facilities paint their Behavioral Safety logo and slogan on plant buildings, such as storage tanks. In some company's observers have also been recognized for their valuable contribution with 'nights out' with their partners at company hosted events.

Some processes also provide 'thank-you' rewards (e.g. vouchers, certificates, etc) to recognize individuals who have identified an important safety problem and fixed it. Sometimes these are awarded by managers and sometimes by the person's peers. If given by managers, they tend to be made at a team or safety meeting recognizing the contribution of the individual.

Sustainability Reviews

Regular performance reviews of the entire process and the performance of the project team *is essential* to sustain the process over the years. Initially, as you rollout the process, reviews tend to take the form of weekly SWOT assessments.

More formal reviews tend to occur every quarter for the first 12 months to examine the process in its entirety, from the performance of the Project Team to observer's data collection to data-analysis and corrective actions completed. Thereafter, formal reviews should be conducted at 6 monthly intervals for the next 24 months. These reviews help to keep the momentum going in the first three years, the critical time period when most Behavioral Safety processes fail, or begin to fail. It is important that the reviews are based on formal objective criteria, so that each review is directly comparable with previous or future reviews. Using a Behavioral Safety scorecard is a big help as it provides focus to the review and helps the company step back to look at the 'big picture'.

Scorecard results provide the impetus for the company to find ways of identifying and addressing any opportunities for change. The example shown in Exhibit 9.9 shows how the effectiveness of the process typically grew each quarter, until it was 'firing on all cylinders' within 12 months. Repeat annual reviews are one of the best ways to maintain a Behavioral Safety process over the long-term. At the same time, it is worth re-issuing any safety surveys, or holding Focus Group exercises to highlight opportunities for change and action still present in the wider safety systems.

Behavioral Safety Performance	Measure	Qtr 1	Qtr 2	Qtr 3	Qtr 4	Comments
Project team	Effectiveness	○	○	●	●	
Project Team Resources	Availability	○	●	●	●	
Checklist Quality	Specific / 20 Behaviors or Less	●	●	●	●	
Observers	% Observation Rate	○	○	●	●	
Quality of Observations	% Related to Incidents	●	●	●	●	
Targets	Difficulty Level	○	○	○	●	
Feedback	# of Methods	●	○	●	●	
Information & Publicity	% Provided & Received	●	○	●	●	
Safety Leadership	% Leadership Score	○	○	●	●	
Visible Ongoing Support	% VOS Score	○	○	●	●	
Data Analysis	% Collated & Analyzed	○	○	●	●	
Corrective Actions	% Completed	●	○	○	●	

Exhibit 9.9: Example Sustainability Review Scorecard

Summary

I have often been asked *'How long does a Behavioral Safety process last?'* My answer has always been the same: *How long do you want it to last?* In other words, how motivated are you to make the process work? How much effort you put in, determines how many years the process will last. The online survey of end-users shows some companies have had their process in place for over 30 years, while others have folded in the first year. The message is that maintaining people's enthusiasm and motivation requires the process to deliver for them. Following the sustainability guidelines offered gives you a fighting chance to do just that.

10 Multi-Site Implementations

A multi-national Oil & Gas company had set ambitious targets for growth in market share and profitability. They had previously implemented a Total Quality Management initiative, which had realized performance improvements but had not produced the 'step-change' it was looking for. Annual Employee Surveys had indicated that managerial leadership skills (e.g. feedback, listening, coaching), were not as effective as they could be, and change was difficult. 'Best Practice Benchmarking' also revealed the company's safety performance offered considerable 'opportunities' for change. The company's leadership developed and communicated three vision objectives: (1) become the industry 'pacesetter' in its core activities; (2) possess the best technology; and (3) be the safest company in the industry. The company worked hard on its strategy and processes, but 'step change' was slow in coming. They realized they needed to focus on leadership behavior. To meet their objectives, they wanted to focus on safety leadership in the belief the associated leadership skills would spill over into other operational areas.

They engaged an advisor with a 'world-class' Behavioral Safety track record and a comprehensive safety leadership process called 'PEER®' (Positively Engaging Employee Risk) to develop a comprehensive 3-year strategy that focused on achieving superior business results through positive safety leadership behaviors. To ensure the strategy was not just seen as a series of 'safety leadership' training exercises, it had to explicitly [a] involve and engage company management team leadership at all levels (i.e., CEO to Front-line Supervisor); [b] promote management team leadership engagement with employees; and [c] involve employees. To meet these goals, every manager in the company was to receive safety leadership training and every facility would implement a comprehensive Behavioral Safety process covering all its safety-related activities.

A Steering Committee was formed, headed by the Chairman as the Executive Sponsor, which included the Safety Director, and the regional Vice Presidents. A set of 10 Key safety leadership principles and a strategic 'roadmap' that aligned PEER® with other business goals was developed. This outlined [1] the requirements for project preparation that outlined the projects goals; [2] an implementation 'blueprint' defining a 'pull & push' rollout strategy (i.e. top-down framework and support, with local level development and implementation); [3] the *development of a 'toolkit' package containing templates, guidelines, standards, and procedures; [4] a final pilot preparation phase to test all the materials, understanding, and implementation; [5] ongoing rollout, support, and maintenance; and [6] evaluation reviews.*

The Corporate Safety department was tasked with being the global focal point and providing implementation support. They developed a 'blueprint' that prioritized the rollout based on assessing each location against the Behavioral Safety Maturity Ladder. Toolkits were developed and customized to suit each country. This included an interlocking PEER® scorecard system established for Executive Board members down to supervisory levels. The Scorecards were aligned with the company's 'Safety Accountability Matrix', the comprehensive Behavioral Safety process, and other business results.

During the rollout, the safety leadership and implementation processes were customized to fit each site's specific safety and business needs. The scorecard results were rolled up at each company level to ensure that the results specified at one level became the key outcome areas that highlighted improvement opportunities to the next level above, and so on. Quarterly reviews were held in each facility to fine tune the processes. The results helped to identify and drive changes to Human Resource, Engineering, Procurement, Process Safety Systems, and Training to support the overall initiative. Over the three years the company's overall incident rate fell by 89 percent, bringing the company to 'world-class' status. With significant savings and productivity benefits the project was hailed as a success.

The above example shows that a global safety leadership training initiative rolled out in conjunction with the implementation of a Behavioral Safety process will reduce incident rates and can improve overall business performance. It is a clever strategy for bringing about transformation and organizational change, simply because people do not 'overtly' object to improving safety. As such, it avoids many of the 'political' objections that can arise with other global strategic initiatives. The above example also structured the process to ensure the objectives were met from a strategic viewpoint. Implementing Behavioral Safety on one site can present significant challenges, but these are multiplied exponentially with multi-site implementations. As illustrated in the above example, a different set of skills, tools, and approaches are required. The key to success is taking a 'birds-eye' view and stamping structure on every aspect before the rollout begins.

Developing Multi-Site Implementations

Multi-site implementations are not easy for a variety of reasons. Common problems are related to 'pushback' arising from competing priorities, limited budgets, insufficient personnel, political issues, unique company cultures (e.g. sales, research and production cultures), and national cultures. Other complications can arise from issues related to joint ventures or associate companies, where corporate control is limited.

In my experience, different national cultures are not that much of a problem provided the process is tailored to suit, and 'cultural' sensitivity is observed at all times. Some of the projects I have been involved in have had tens of thousands of workers representing as many as 60 different nationalities working on site. The major problems come from competing priorities, limited budgets, 'lean' manpower levels, and initiative overload, particularly where there is misalignment between the various ongoing projects. In these circumstances, common questions that arise include: Why are we doing this? Who's paying? What are the project goals? What do we have to do? How can we align initiatives? And what are the benefits?

It requires careful thought, therefore, about executive level sponsorship; senior level oversight; in-depth planning; development of the right materials; allocation of the right resources; and a strong and purposeful rollout and execution.

Develop a Strategic Roadmap

Strategy development is of the highest priority for successful multi-site implementations as it provides the framework and bedrock on which everything else rests. Creating a 'Strategic Roadmap' is essential as it helps to provide a visible indicator of 'where you are going' and 'how you are going to get there'. These 'Roadmaps' usually encompass five stages: [1] initiate; [2] plan; [3] execute; [4] control; and [5] close.

Each major element of the 'roadmap' must be converted into specific behaviors that are defined, enacted, measured, and reinforced. Quantifiable measures must be in place and aligned with the behaviors you need / desire. In this way people can understand and articulate the components of the Behavioral Safety change process that are 'above the line': i.e. 'walk the walk' and 'talk the talk'. In other words, the strategy should be translated into concrete operational terms.

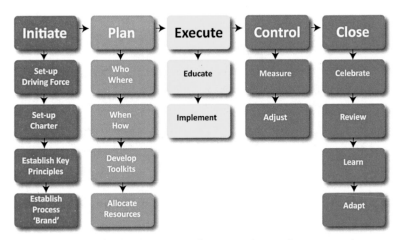

Exhibit 10.1: Example Strategic Roadmap

Initiate

The first stage of setting up a multi-site implementation is the 'Initiate' stage. Here considerations are given to developing a supportive infrastructure to provide the necessary driving force, establishing key principles and 'branding' the process. The driving force behind multi-site implementations is usually an executive sponsor, an oversight Steering Committee, and an implementation Task Force. For smaller-scale projects the Steering Committee and Task Force can be one and the same.

Executive Sponsor

Establishing a multi-site Behavioral Safety process within a business is only viable if it has long-term, high level executive support and visibility, accompanied by an information 'dashboard' for monitoring its effectiveness. In others words, a strategic approach to deploying Behavioral Safety across multiple locations must start at the top. This helps to create credibility for the process that extends throughout the entire company.

Large-scale strategic change initiatives are notorious for not delivering. Some research suggests that only 7 percent achieve 100 percent of their objectives, with most delivering 75 percent or less. One of the key success factors is the active participation and oversight role of an Executive Sponsor. In terms of effectiveness the best sponsors ensure that [1] all strategic options are considered before the project is approved; [2] the project is assured of receiving all the necessary resources; and [3] the project team has the necessary authority to accomplish the projects goals.

In terms of assuring delivery of the objectives, the sponsor ensures that the [1] project business case is sound; [2] right people are in place and are held accountable for realizing the benefits; and [3] technical specifications and Key Performance Indicators (KPI's) will make the business case achievable.

Executive sponsors also actively take part in establishing the Behavioral Safety implementation goals and priorities. They provide the resources necessary to achieving the agreed upon goals and explicitly communicate the importance of Behavioral Safety to everyone in the company. Other activities include providing timely support when internal blockages prevent goal achievement, and making themselves available to 'sell' the process when necessary.

Steering Committee

Multi-site implementations usually require a corporate level 'Steering Committee' to help plan, implement, and evaluate the 'rollout'. The advantage is the Steering Committee helps to bring about a consistency of purpose, focus, and execution, and become the focal point for the rollout 'Task Force' to report progress and/or roadblocks. As such, the committee adds value by clearing the path for introducing the Behavioral Safety process into the company across the sites.

As a minimum the Steering Committee should comprise of an executive level sponsor, a project manager (usually a high level HSE function), a Behavioral Safety expert/specialist, and high-level regional managers where the process is to be introduced.

It is a good idea for the Steering Committee to develop a charter that specifies [1] its purpose (e.g. take responsibility for the feasibility, business case and oversight of the achievement of outcomes); [2] the roles of each member (e.g. provide support and guidance for the implementation Task Force); and [3] the format of meetings and its agenda (e.g. review project status against the objectives).

Implementation Task Force

An implementation Task Force should also be set up to complete all the day-to-day work required to bring the project to fruition. The Task Force reports to the Steering Committee and generally comprises members of the Corporate Safety or Loss Control departments. Both the Corporate Safety Manager and the Behavioral Safety expert are also members of the Task Force, to provide a link between it and the Steering Committee. In essence, the Task Force becomes the driver and the main focal point for business sites to refer to in terms of requesting support, reporting progress, and/or dealing with roadblocks. If the multi-site implementation crosses international borders or different time zones, there may be a case for setting up 'regional' Task Forces that report to the Corporate Task Force.

Establish Key Principles

Usually developed by the Steering Committee, the purpose of establishing the key principles is to outline the base philosophy of the implementation. In turn, these help to establish the specific objectives of the implementation that collectively guide the planning and rollout. For example, to achieve excellence in Behavioral Safety one of the major goals is to create a genuine 'safety partnership' between management and employees. To make this more concrete a set of key principles would be developed. These might be:

1) Involve and engage company management team leadership at all levels of the Organization (i.e., CEO to Front-line Supervisor).
2) Promote management team leadership engagement with employees.
3) Involve all employees in the safety improvement effort.

Enacting these key principles might include setting the following objectives:

a) All managers EHS leadership behaviors to be determined by the appropriate managerial levels developed into self-observation checklists and monitored weekly.
b) All managers will conduct at least 2 X PEER type observations / engagements weekly.
c) Managers monitor weekly Corrective Action Rate.
d) All employees help to construct focused observation checklists.
e) Most safety observations will be workgroup based.
f) All workgroups set own safety improvement targets.
g) Management will ensure the process delivers focused feedback to all.
h) Sites implement a 'local' Behavioral Safety marketing / publicity campaign using the corporate 'brand' materials.
i) All site contractors implement some form of Behavioral Safety system, with progress reported to local company management on a regular basis.

The key principles and objectives also provide the means for the Steering Committee and the Task Force to set clear expectations and communicate in one voice so that a consistent message is achieved and transmitted throughout the company. It is a good idea to build your marketing efforts around the principles and objectives, so that communications are not diluted or subverted as the project is rolled out to the different regions and/or sites.

Branding the Process

Selling the process is absolutely vital to success and is a never-ending activity. Naming and branding the process can be an enormous help as it provides a common reference point that can be used in marketing efforts when selling the process into different business units. Other benefits are that the corporate body retains control over the branding of all products and materials developed to support the initiative. It is often a good idea to seek the assistance of the corporate Public Relations and/or Communication Departments, as their marketing infrastructure tends to already be in place.

Developing a 'Brand' name can take some effort; it should be simple, memorable, and unique. The Shell *'Hearts & Minds'* campaign is a good example of a brand name that is simple to remember and also specifies what it is trying to do. Sometimes, holding a competition to name a global or multi-site initiative is a good way to start involving people in the process. It may also be possible to use an existing internal brand name for an existing safety initiative, provided it has a good reputation and is highly regarded; otherwise you run the risk of tarnishing the new Behavioral Safety process with a 'brand' name already in disrepute.

Planning

The planning stage should follow Rudyard Kipling's 1902 poem *'The Elephant Child'* that examines 'the who, the what, the where, the when, the how, and the why' to develop an implementation 'blueprint'. The idea is to link the key principles and their objectives with the core activities of the process and the expected outcomes. This requires serious consideration of resource requirements, rollout strategy, and time frames.

Who and Where

At this stage, the *'what'* is the Behavioral Safety process, and the *'why'* is to reduce incident rates, and create a 'safety partnership'. So our attentions are turned first to 'who is to be involved and where'? Basically, this aspect identifies the scope of the exercise. Are you going to include all business units, or just some? If some, when is the remainder to be included? This is important as this determines the required infrastructure and resource allocation. For example if you are crossing international boundaries, there is likely to be language and cultural issues to be catered for.

Exhibit 10.2: Inter-Linked Planning Considerations

There are two ways of prioritizing the 'who and the where' for the rollout. The first is to be guided by a site's incident rates: i.e. develop a company league table and rank the business units according to their lost-time and total recordable incident rates. Those with highest incident rates would be targeted first. The second is to use the Behavioral Safety Maturity Ladder (see chapter 2) to identify and target those at the 'Beginning' and 'Developing' stages as prime candidates for initial rollout. Simultaneously, other units could use the Behavioral Safety Maturity Ladder to enhance their existing processes until they reach the 'Excelling' stage. Of course, it may prove useful to use both methods.

One of the features to success is to identify the key influencers at each level in the company who can help to sell the process into the various sites. Identifying these people will depend on the purpose of their role. For example, is their role to be 'political backers', 'end-users', or both? Inevitably, political backing from influential people will be required, and these may not be the same people as the 'end-users'. Consider 'Who' these people are, and 'Why' these people are considered helpful. This will revolve around identifying those who have the relevant experience, expertise and interest to assist in the rollout. Decisions then need to be made about how to involve them.

For example, do you want them to become a Steering Committee member in their region, or do you want to use their site(s) as pilots? In other words, be clear about want you want from them before seeking their assistance.

When & How

Once the 'Who & Where' is known, attention is paid to 'When and How' the rollout is to be executed. The 'When' refers to the timing of the rollout. This will obviously be dependent on having all your 'ducks in a row', but a target date could be set to focus people's attention on delivery, the resources, development of toolkits, etc., to avoid letting the project rollout 'drift' indefinitely.

The 'How' is probably the most difficult aspect of the planning as you want people to willingly 'buy-in' to the initiative. From a strategic perspective there are three routes, each with their own advantages and disadvantages: [1] independent implementation; [2] centrally developed 'template' with local rollouts; and, [3] sequential 'pull & push' rollouts.

Independent implementations are usually based on a simple corporate instruction to business units to adopt and implement a Behavioral Safety initiative. The advantages could be an optimal, tailored process for each unit with no central coordination required, which may reduce resistance from the unit to corporate edicts. The downside is each unit could re-invent the wheel, increasing the time and effort involved. Depending on the Behavioral Safety approach adopted, there could also be inconsistencies of approaches between the sites resulting in different reporting metrics (i.e. scorecards)

Centrally developed 'template' rollouts can provide consistency and a uniformity of processes across the entire business with a single, central development cost, and perhaps reduced maintenance costs. However, central coordination is required, while building in 'flexibility' to cater for 'local' needs. A supportive infrastructure may also be required in each region to liaise between the corporate 'Task Force' and local business units. This strategy may also meet with political resistance as corporate is perceived to be 'pushing' Behavioral Safety onto a site, who may not feel they want it, or are not ready for it.

Sequential 'Pull & Push' rollouts refer to a top-down 'push' from corporate to nudge sites into implementing Behavioral Safety, while 'pull' comes from a local 'bottom-up' desire to implement. This is probably the most realistic approach for large multi-nationals as some business units are already likely to be doing some form of Behavioral Safety. These could assess themselves against the Behavioral Safety Maturity Ladder, and determine what level they are at and what actions they could take to improve their process. Some of the lessons learned from these 'early adopters' could also be incorporated into the overall strategy, and can also serve as role models for other sites.

The advantage of the *'pull & push'* approach is its explicit recognition that different units will be at different maturity levels (see chapter 2), and each level requires different levels of assistance. In this way, Corporate can 'keep a light hand on the tiller' by providing the framework, toolkits, and other resources, while allowing sites to go at their own pace within the allotted time-frame. Those who need assistance can receive it, while those who feel able and capable of 'doing their own thing' in light of local circumstances can do so with minimal assistance. It is essential, however, to support and guide those who enthusiastically run ahead of the pack. It is also imperative that the reporting metrics (i.e. scorecards) are standardized for all business units so the Steering Committee can compare 'apples with apples', and keep track of the overall status of implementation and results.

Develop Toolkits

Once the rollout strategy has been determined, the next step is to develop high quality 'Toolkits' for use in the various locations. What these comprise of is going to be determined by the Behavioral Safety approach adopted. At the very least this must include implementation guidelines and standards for project teams, training materials, and various templates with specific examples that can be readily used. Providing simple and easy 'Toolkits' so that business units can make the tools fit the local environment is recommended. Lessons learned from the Shell *'Hearts and Minds'* campaign suggest any tools developed should [1] be small, micro-tools, designed to alter behavior; [2] documented on few pages; [3] fit with day-to-day activities such as safety meetings and toolbox talks; [4] designed to be used by managers, supervisors and crews; [5] based on facts about human behavior; and [6] be professionally designed and presented in a bright and fun way. Collectively, the 'Toolkits' help to ensure that the overall strategy is followed and minimizes dilution, adaptation, or subverting of the process beyond the set guidelines.

The toolkit topics should target three aspects: [1] project teams and their roles; [2] observers; and [3] reporting criteria.

Project Team Toolkits could cover:
- Team Roles / Reporting relationships
- Developing a Steering Committee charter
- Designing a process (the chosen type)
- Data-mining techniques
- Developing checklists (safety leadership, self-observation, outcomes, behaviors)
- Training Observers
- Day-to-day process management
- Collating and analyzing data
- Monitoring the process for 'tripwires'
- Reviewing & adapting the process

Observers Toolkits should include:
- Field Observation techniques (how to observe)
- Verbal feedback and coaching skills
- Facilitating feedback meetings
- Setting improvement targets
- Reporting corrective actions

Reporting 'Toolkits' should specify the 'Key Performance Indicators' to be used to monitor the effectiveness of the process and its expected achievements. For example, 95 percent of all corrective actions completed within 30 days. In addition, the Task Force should prepare and distribute a process 'Scorecard' that includes the Key Performance Indicators of interest so that all data reported upwards would be consistent at each layer, to provide a 'big picture' view of sites, regions, divisions, etc., that would be directly comparable.

It may also prove useful to use the development of these 'Toolkits' to align the process with other safety objectives and methods. For example, developing equivalent 'Toolkits' for JSA's, Tailgate or Toolbox talks and the like under the same 'Branding' to help reinforce the message the process is not just a passing fad, but an integral part of the company's overall safety effort.

Resource Allocation

Inevitably, a multi-site implementation will require considerable resources to be allocated. This will include budgeting for pre-implementation planning, project management staffing costs, training, marketing, publication, travel, contracting costs, (if any) and actual implementation costs.

Aspects to consider include allocating a 'seed' budget for any 'pilot' projects (sites may not have budgeted for implementation and corporate may need to assist) to help convince the remaining sites that the Behavioral Safety process provides benefits. There will certainly be a 'training budget' required for developing internal company 'trainers' in the geographical regions, who in turn may be required to travel to various locations to train 'on-site' personnel. Travel budgets will also be required for corporate 'Task Force' members to provide on-site training, assistance or sustainability reviews. A marketing budget will be required for promoting the process across the company, while publications costs will include the development, publication and distribution of the 'Toolkits'. As these examples show, it is vital to ensure there is a sufficient resource allocation to ensure the process can be planned, implemented, and maintained, within the required time scales. Although, the initial costs may be extensive, these are usually recouped from substantial cost-savings arising from injury reductions and increased production.

Execute

Strategic rollout and execution entails educating the sites to provide them with the necessary skills to successfully implement the process. In the first instance this will likely take the form of training the trainers. If possible, it is often cost-effective to bring all the potential trainers to one location and train them together. The benefits are that each has been trained in the same way so the message is not diluted. These people usually 'bond' over the course of the training period, and create a 'self-support' network, where each person can turn to others for ongoing help and guidance.

Each of the trainers then return to their site locations, help sell the process into the sites, and train 'on-site' personnel in their respective roles. It is essential there is some form of quality control built in at this stage (e.g. competency outcomes are specified and assessed). This could include certification of successfully completing and 'understanding' the training and content. The trainer also becomes the 'on-site' coach to mentor the project team through its paces as it rolls-out the process across the entire site.

Site rollout and execution (see chapter 8) should follow a site-specific implementation plan (see chapter 5) developed by the site's project team. Initially it may prove useful to use a 'pilot' business unit in each geographical location. This can facilitate testing of all the Toolkit materials, people's understanding of these, and the process design to learn lessons prior to proceeding with the 'main' rollout. This also offers the advantages of ensuring the trainers are competent, the materials are readily understood, are suitable for different cultures, and the supportive 'Task Force' infrastructure is in place and working as intended.

Control

Any process needs internal controls to ensure it is working as intended. Developing a cascaded Scorecard system is one of the better control methods. In essence, the system touches each organization level of the company and provides the necessary feedback that keeps everybody informed to help maintain progress.

Each month the 'Scorecard' for each level is rolled up by department, site, region, etc., until it reaches the corporate Task Force in the 'mother ship'. In this way, people at each layer in the company are involved in keeping track of the project. Each layer can also take a 'birds eye' view of progress that is relevant to them. This offers the advantage of any corrective actions being resolved at the local level before any issues are escalated to the Task Force.

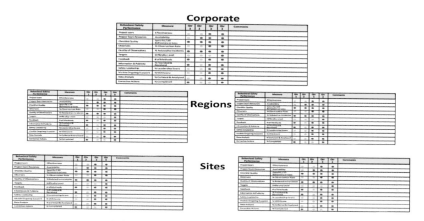

Exhibit 10.3: Cascaded Scorecard System

The Task Force uses the scorecards to highlight successes and any opportunities for change from a 'big picture' view that are reported to the Steering Committee. The process can then be adapted in light of current knowledge to ensure the process remains viable and sustainable across the company.

Closing the Rollout

A major milestone has been hit once the process has been successfully rolled-out across all the intended sites. This achievement changes the function of the role of the corporate Task Force to one of maintaining and sustaining the process (see chapter 9).

Celebrate

This is also the time to start celebrating successes from a corporate perspective. First, acknowledge and recognize the contribution of the Task Force for bringing the project to fruition. Second, highlight any successes spinning out of each site's Behavioral Safety process. Both can, and should, be bought together in company newsletters and other materials using the previously developed marketing infrastructure.

Review

The next stage is to review both the effectiveness of the project rollout and conduct sustainability reviews on each site (see chapter 9). In terms of the project rollout the purpose is to identify and document what went right and where opportunities for improvement exist. This provides a living document for other teams that may be 'rolling-out' other initiatives and for others who may join the Task Force.

The review should focus on [1] the use of resources; [2] scheduling; [3] quality and uptake of 'branded' materials; [4] the trainers effectiveness 'on-the-ground'; [5] the reception of the process on sites; [6] factors that helped implementation; and, [7] factors that hindered implementation. Task Force members in conjunction with local 'trainers' should also conduct periodic sustainability process reviews on site.

Lessons learned

The project rollout review should finish with a 'lessons learned' document. In essence this should highlight what worked well and what should be done differently in similar projects. It is useful to develop a short and simple 'lessons learned' document. For example:

Lesson Type: Data
Road Map Footprint: Control / Measure
Nature of Event: Scorecard data not being attended too.
Impact level: High
Noted Lesson: Rolled up Scorecard data did not always accurately portray 'state of play' in two regions. Many actions not being attended to derailed the process. A significant amount of training and rework was required to bring process back on track. The root cause was a lack of regular process reviews, triggered by change out of project personnel. In hindsight, project personnel changes should be reported back to the Task Force so alternative arrangements can be made to ensure succession planning.

The documents should be placed in an easily accessible central project 'depository', perhaps using Excel or an SQL database. In this way, if there are project team personnel changes or new sites are bought into the company there will be a continuity mechanism for passing on the projects history.

Adapt

Tracking both the outcomes of the sustainability reviews and lessons learned facilitates 'course corrections' over a period of time to help ensure the entire process is maintained and delivers the expected outcomes. Again, this requires a consistency of effort over the years. A time will come when the process is deeply embedded in each site and a 'normal' part of their daily routines. Once this stage is reached and oversight is no longer necessary, the Task Force can be reduced in size or disbanded.

Summary

Multi-site or global implementations are a huge under-taking and a company should be prepared for the long haul. The Steering Committee and Task Force should be in place to help nurture the process in each site until such time as the process is simply a normal way of doing business.

Typical problems that will be encountered are failure to get 'buy-in' from management and employees; a failure in regular measurement and communication about performances between the Task Force and the sites; and/or a failure to acknowledge and recognize good performance. With good planning and a strategic roadmap many of the issues can be overcome leading to successful implementation on a 'grand scale'.

11 Short-Term Maintenance Implementations

A petrochemical company had been implementing Behavioral Safety with good results for a while and site management wanted to adapt the process to suit a major six week plant shutdown due in nine months time. The Behavioral Safety coordinator attended a series of 'lessons learned' seminars with senior managers and shutdown planners, so that the process could be planned. As a result of the seminars, the tender documentation required all Contractors to implement Behavioral Safety.

Pre-shutdown preparations included developing an Induction package for the tradesmen and an equivalent briefing package for Contractor Management. The Behavioral Safety coordinator examined the injury database for previous shutdowns and developed a Safety Observation checklist specific to shutdown activities. He also worked with the shutdown management team to develop a safety leadership checklist containing ten behaviors. These were used by management during the six-week pre-preparation phase. With no pre-shutdown incidents recorded, the shutdown management team was optimistic about the prospects for an incident free shutdown. To encourage area ownership the site was divided into ten observation zones, with three managers assigned to those areas throughout the duration of the shutdown phase. As the shutdown phase approached, contractor and company observers were trained.

To achieve a 1:10 ratio, with a shutdown workforce of over 3500 contractor personnel, 300 observers were provided by the 12 contractor companies a few days before the shutdown commencement and trained. They were also shown the site induction package for comment, which resulted in some minor revisions, which were completed before the main body of contractor personnel arrived on site. The first four days observation data was used to set an improvement target for each of the ten observation areas. Over the next 45 days, feedback was delivered at 'tailgate' talks before work started. Overall, 12,400 safety observations and 1200 managerial safety leadership walk rounds were conducted and over 250 corrective actions completed. With an excess of 1.9 million man-hours worked during the shutdown phase, the Total Recordable Incident Rate was 0.21. A post-shutdown review led to the Behavioral Safety process being formally incorporated into the shutdown planning section of the safety management system manual.

Plant shutdowns for scheduled and unscheduled major maintenance work are complex, costly, and difficult to manage and are potentially very dangerous. Such abnormal operations are a classic time for people to get hurt: tight schedules, crowded work areas, and shift work are all aspects that raise serious concerns about safety. Condensed processes have helped improve safety performance during these times, but forward planning is essential.

Two key aspects that are crucial for safe shutdowns are managerial engagement and the involvement of contractor personnel. A well planned, designed, and executed Behavioral Safety process can deliver both. However, a condensed application of the process, provides many challenges that requires a consistency of purpose, application, and execution from all parties involved, including [1] shutdown planners; [2] contractor management and personnel; [3] the behavioral safety project team; [4] operations management and personnel; and [5] EHS department and personnel.

Behavioral Safety shutdown implementations generally consist of four stages: [1] the preparation stage; [2] the design stage; [3] the implementation stage; and [4] the review stage.

The Preparation Stage

The preparation stage is the period of time in which the project team gathers the information required to plan the implementation.

Most pre-planned shutdowns start with a series of managerial seminars involving plant and contractor management and the shutdown planning team. The purpose is to highlight lessons learned from previous shutdowns and ensure the challenges are addressed. This is a good time for the Behavioral Safety Project team to have an input into the planning process, set key principles, and integrate the process with other safety activities.

One of the main actions is to have the Behavioral Safety process entered into the shutdown tender documentation by the contracts department. This can be in the tenders 'scope of works' if the contractors are to manage their own process; or in the shutdown safety plan if the site project team is going to manage the process and include the contractors. This helps to avoid contractual issues at a later stage, where contractors may want to 'cross-charge' the plant for associated labor costs. I once calculated the percent of time taken by the entire Behavioral Safety process (observations, feedback meetings, etc.) on a construction project was less than 0.23 percent of the total project hours. Although minuscule, I have come across many contractor companies who want to charge the client for implementing Behavioral Safety as an extra, because it was not specified in the original contract document.

Shutdown Planning

The Behavioral Safety project team should obtain information about the schedule of works, the nature of the tasks being undertaken and when, so that they can develop the process accordingly. Ideally, this will be done in conjunction with the shutdown planners at the very start, and at regular meetings leading up to the shutdown stage. At a minimum, the schedule of works should include contractor briefings, observation time, and feedback or tailgate meetings. This helps to avoid time 'crunches', during the actual shutdown period when everyone is heavily concerned with maintaining the schedule.

The specific information required from the shutdown planning department includes identifying the contractors involved, the contact details of key personnel, the plant areas where each contractor will be working, how many of their personnel will be involved and how long they will be on site.

The Design Stage

The design stage involves many activities including [1] identifying the observation areas or 'zones'; [2] determining how many observers are required or wanted; [3] determining how many plant managers will be available; [4] developing shutdown specific checklists; [5] organizing training venues; [6] working out how feedback will be given to people; [7] developing a Behavioral Safety element to the induction process.

Identify Observation Zones

In the same way as site maps are used to decide on observation areas or 'zones' in normal Behavioral Safety processes (see chapter 5), the plant or facility is divided so that observers and managers can be assigned to specific areas to encourage 'area ownership'. This helps in three ways. The first is that it creates continuity, in that managers become familiar with the people, the area and the issues throughout the shutdown stage. The second is that it becomes possible to identify the minimum number of observers required for the shutdown. The third is that it facilitates data collation and analysis.

Identifying the Number of Observers

Identifying the number of observers often depends on the observation approach adopted. If a 'One-on-One, Peer-to-Peer' approach is adopted, the rule of thumb is ten percent of the entire shutdown workforce. Workgroup approaches tend to need fewer observers, usually one or two per observation area. Many shutdowns are 24/7, usually with a day and night crew. So for each area the numbers of observers must be doubled to give an overall number. Some highly successful incident free shutdowns have only had 28-30 observers for 3,500 shutdown workers, covering 14 observation zones. The number required needs to be transmitted to each of the shutdown contractors so they can make the appropriate provisions. Of course, a mix of both observation approaches may be appropriate.

Identifying the Number of Managers Available

During shutdowns, there should be many plant managers available, as by definition they will not be doing their normal job. Though some may be assigned to training courses or on vacation, the remainder should be assigned to an observation area, so they can conduct observations and hold 'safety conversations' with people. In some shutdowns we have assigned at least two plant managers and one HSE person to an area for the duration of the shutdown. They usually coordinate their visits to the observation areas amongst themselves. *The most important aspect is that each manager visits the observation area on a daily basis.* I have seen many incident free shutdowns when this occurs. In subsequent shutdowns on the same site, these same managers have not been as diligent, and many people have been hurt.

Developing Shutdown Specific Safety Checklists

Developing shutdown checklists is based on data-mining techniques (see chapter 6) of any previous shutdown incident and near-hit records. If possible, these should include contractor records as well as those of the plants. Once the critical categories of behavior have been identified, a decision needs to be made about which types of checklist to develop (see chapter 7). If the checklist is to be a generic shutdown checklist to cover all activities, then it is possible to simply use the incident data results to cover the critical behaviors identified. Often these involve issues surrounding Access and Egress, Use of Tools & Equipment, Housekeeping, and Use of Personal Protective Equipment (PPE).

If job specific checklists are to be developed, the shutdown schedule of works should be examined. I have previously used the shutdown job number and the associated activities to develop these. The advantage is that it becomes possible to identify exactly which jobs have been completed safely, and which jobs are commonly associated with unsafe behaviors. This approach takes more effort, but in my view is extremely useful, as any 'unsafe' issues can be planned for, in the next shutdown. In one shutdown for example, four workers were moving an 18 inch 'slip plate' by hand into a position below the chain block for insertion into the line being hydro tested. When the guys lowered the slip plate to the ground, one of them had the tip of his finger crushed. At the next shutdown, explicit provision was made for all slip plates to be removed and inserted with lifting equipment.

Regardless of the type of checklist developed, these should be forwarded to the appropriate contractors for comment. This gives an opportunity for them to add or refine the checklists and begin to take ownership of them. It also allows them to begin training their workforce about some of the safety issues seen as important by the client during the shutdown period, so people arrive on site with some pre-preparation.

Developing Shutdown Specific Safety Leadership Checklists

Demonstrable safety leadership is vital throughout any shutdown, although the safety leadership behaviors are likely to be somewhat different than for normal plant operations. In most instances, the same safety leadership checklists can be used for all managers. These should be developed in conjunction with a representative group of managers and forwarded to others for comment, including contractor management.

Auditor:	Area:	Date from:	Date to:		
Have YOU as a manager (a 'leader of safety') completed the following within the period identified above?				Yes	No
1. Provide support to daily tool-box talks in my designated area					
2. Attended the daily meetings in my designated area & also the management meeting					
3. Completed any commitments I have on the audit schedule & offered help if others cannot complete theirs					
4. Held a safety conversation with a tradesman on the plant					
5. Spoken with my direct reports about safety activities in their control					
6. Helped to close out any remedial actions within my designated area with the Area Eng.					
7. Owned & actioned and solved a specific safety issue within my designated area					
8. Completed my Visual Ongoing Support if applicable					
9. Held a discussion on plant about a risk assessment (WCP, JSA, Supervisor's ...etc)					
10. Reviewed the Near Miss book within my designated area					
Totals					
*My percentage score for this checklist (Total = Yes / Yes + No * 100)*					%

Exhibit 11.1: Example Shutdown Safety Leadership Checklist

Organizing Training Venues

Training venues can be a problem on shutdowns simply because of the sheer number of personnel arriving on site and the different types of training required (e.g. inductions, safety training, etc). The project team should arrange the training schedule and venue in advance with the shutdown HSE team.

The venue should be used to provide briefings to contractor management and training of observers. One of the project team should also be involved in the Behavioral Safety aspect of the induction process when the bulk of personnel arrive on site.

It is common for some people to not be on site for training on the appointed day, so it is a good idea to cater for this by scheduling a couple of extra training days.

Giving Feedback

From the Behavioral Safety projects teams' point of view, they have to develop the means to provide daily work area feedback to shutdown personnel, and to the shutdown management team (see chapter 9). This is probably the most difficult and time-consuming aspect of the process. Data has to be entered, collated, and analyzed in real time. Usually, project team members will work 12-hour shifts, with the day observations entered during night shifts and night shift observations entered by day shift personnel. The idea is to ensure the feedback for each work area or zone is ready for the start of the next shift. The information is usually discussed at 'tailgate' meetings.

The project team also has to ensure that the shutdown team receives appropriate summary information, and any important trends. Usually there are daily managerial meetings that can be used. On some shutdowns, it is common for all safety personnel from the facility and the contractors to meet on a daily basis to highlight important safety issues. Both of these are good avenues to pass on progress updates.

It is also a good idea to place large graphical feedback boards presenting the trends in the Percent Safe score at the site entrance and other strategic locations. These should be updated daily, so that personnel can see the shutdown's overall performance trend over the shutdown period.

Some create a daily shutdown specific safety newsletter that is distributed to everyone. This is an excellent medium to transmit more detailed information about safety in general and the Behavioral Safety process in particular. Some of the better ones publish a shutdown EHS performance report that keeps a tally of the number and types of incidents, how many Behavioral Safety observations and Near-hit reports have been turned in, and report the sites overall Percent Safe score. They also include pictures of personnel, run safety crossword competitions, highlight particularly safe workers, or ask for nominations of the best 'safety conscious' supervisors and so on. In essence these use social recognition as a means to keep peoples interest in ongoing safety events and performance.

Create an Induction Package

Many contractors coming onto site, may not have heard of Behavioral Safety, or may not be familiar with the approach being used on the shutdown. Some of my clients have developed ten-minute videos showing people being observed and given feedback or coaching, using plant personnel or existing long-term contractors. Others have developed PowerPoint slides. What they all have in common is they specify why Behavioral Safety is being used, how it works and what is expected of people. Each person usually has a takeaway in the form of a Behavioral Safety process briefing leaflet.

With many contract workers, trust is a big issue. Many fear they could be thrown off site if they are observed working unsafely. Others fear reprisals from their management if they are seen to 'rock the boat'. In one instance, for example, an employee made a suggestion to improve the effectiveness of wearing body harnesses, but then hurriedly stated that he wished he had not said anything. When asked why, he replied that if the client decided to take up his suggestion it would mean that his contractor company would have to supply them with the relevant equipment. He would then be seen by his management as the instigator of this additional cost and as such would be victimized. Not naming individuals as part of the Behavioral Safety process, therefore, is a key part of the message that has to be hammered home to all, to make people feel safe so they can become involved.

The induction process also provides an opportunity to ask everyone if they wish to become an observer. Often, one or two people per induction session will volunteer, over and above those needed. These people should be catered for and encouraged.

The Implementation Stage

This is the stage where everything comes together. There will be teething problems as people arrive on site and the project team settle into their routines. A shutdown implementation presents many challenges to Behavioral Safety project teams. Initially, there is a lot of energy expended, which reduces as the project team gets into their stride. Depending on the length of the shutdown, it is not unusual for project team members to be exhausted (especially if they have done their job properly) by the last few days of the shutdown. However, a classic time for injuries to occur is when a project winds down. It is at this point the project team has to dig into their energy reserves and become even more energetic than usual to fight complacency (particularly if no incidents have occurred).

Training observers prior to the shutdown commencement, during the shutdown pre-preparation stage is the first step. Depending on the number of observers, this is usually conducted in the week before the shutdown work actually occurs. Live practice is conducted on the plant itself, as people will be working either in bringing the plant down, or in preparations.

The next step is to conduct the Behavioral Safety inductions as shutdown personnel arrive on site, and enter observation data as it is handed to the project team. It is also likely that training of other volunteer observers takes place during this period.

The third step is to ensure the analyzed data is given in a timely fashion to the observers or their supervisors, for discussion at tailgate meetings. There should be follow-up checks to ensure the feedback data is being discussed as intended. In one shutdown, we discovered that the information was often read out to people but no discussions took place. In others, no mention at all was made of the Behavioral Safety feedback. Although difficult, the project team members should try to attend as many tailgate talks as they can on a random basis and prompt discussion where it is not taking place.

It is also very important to keep a watchful eye on the number of managers visiting their 'designated' observation areas. Some managers will be very diligent, others less so. Often a daily e-mail reminder helps.

Another activity is to pass on the Behavioral Safety information to the person(s) developing the shutdown 'newsletter'. Often, the person is one of the shutdowns HSE people attending the daily meetings, which present the ideal opportunity. The project team should highlight any opportunities for celebration resulting from overall performance (e.g. meeting targets, highlighting behaviors reported as 100 percent safe, etc).

Other activities will inevitably involve coaching observers in the field and ensuring 'corrective actions' are attended to by the appropriate person.

The Review Stage

After a brief rest, a post-shutdown review of the planning, design and implementation stages should be undertaken and recorded. The findings should be presented to the HSE and shutdown planning departments, in addition to the senior management team. This should highlight what went well, what could and should be done differently, and present all the major successes.

Summary

Shutdown overhauls, or other types of abnormal operations are a classic time for incident rates to climb. Implementations applied to facility overhauls are condensed and complex versions of a normal Behavioral Safety process. High levels of coordination are required before and during the overhaul, to ensure everyone is in alignment. Start with the initial planning of the overhaul, so planners can build in the specifications for contractors. Thereafter, the planning and development process proceeds as normal. The real hard work begins on the day of the overhaul, when everything comes together. Be prepared to be flexible and adaptable to suit changing circumstances.

12 Case Histories

In 1989, I was engaged as part of a team to research Behavioral Safety in the British Construction Industry, on behalf of the British Health & Safety Executive (HSE), at the University of Manchester Institute for Science & Technology (UMIST). This was the first time the approach had ever been used in Britain and was conducted in two stages: from 1989-1992 the method was tested on six sites by the team designing checklists and carrying out the observations. Feedback consisted of public graphical charts placed on each of the sites. The second stage was carried out from 1992-1995, on 26 sites, where implementation responsibility was transferred to the construction companies. This culminated in two pioneering research reports for the British HSE. The first showed that Behavioral Safety had considerable merit as a method for helping to improve construction site safety, but its effectiveness was dependent upon site management's commitment. The second, implemented by construction companies under guidance from the research team, showed companies were capable of implementing the approach themselves, with visible management commitment accounting for about 51 percent of the behavioral improvements.

During this time, I also began to implement Behavioral Safety in the chemical industry. Various other opportunities also presented themselves in other industrial sectors, such as Agrochemicals, Petrochemicals, Foods, Metal Refining, Oil & Gas, Paper and Steel. Many of the client companies were concerned to ensure the process was streamlined as much as possible to keep training and time costs to a minimum. The HSE research, and early implementations revealed that the workgroup approach was the most cost-effective as it reduced the need for large number of observers. It also meant that data collation and analyses was more easily managed, when compared to the 'one-on-one, peer-to-peer' approaches that were on offer from other advisors. The following representative case histories stretch from 1992 to the present and illustrate how consistently effective the workgroup approach is in a wide range of settings.

Cellophane Manufacturer

A subsidiary of Courtaulds, a multi-national company manufactured Cellophane film with a 540-person workforce on a continuous three-shift system. With a robust safety management system in place, safety committees and a hazard spotting program, and 30 percent of capital expenditure being spent to address safety issues they thought they were on their way to great safety performance. However, a significant upturn in the number and severity of injuries had them worried. Site personnel told management that many of the incidents were related to people's unsafe behavior. They had heard about the HSE research in the construction industry and contacted the author.

Assessment Survey

The project began with a safety perception survey to discover what the underlying issues might be. This revealed many management system issues were causing problems that led people to behave unsafely to overcome them. Management rapidly took corrective action with the system issues and also decided to try a Behavioral Safety approach.

Process Development

A series of two-hour briefings were held with all the managers on site to obtain their support and buy-in for the process. These spelt out the philosophy of the approach and how the process would be rolled-out. Managers were also asked to recruit an observer from each shift and work area.

Draft checklists containing specific safe behaviors were developed for 14 departments from an analysis of the previous two years incident records. The workforce approved these before 48 volunteer observers attended two day training courses. During the training, the checklists were trialed and refined. The observers practiced using these over the next two weeks. At the end of this period large A3 copies of the checklists were posted in each of the departments so everyone was aware of the safety behaviors being monitored.

The observers monitored their colleagues on the plant for 10-20 minutes a day for four weeks, to establish a baseline of how safely people were working. The baseline average was then used by each of the shift teams to set a safety improvement target. Observers continued to monitor daily and gave feedback when observing people and presented tabulated data at weekly feedback meetings. Corrective actions, followed up by the project team were reported back to the workgroups. This cycle of checklist development, observer training and setting new targets with regular feedback was repeated every 20 weeks or so.

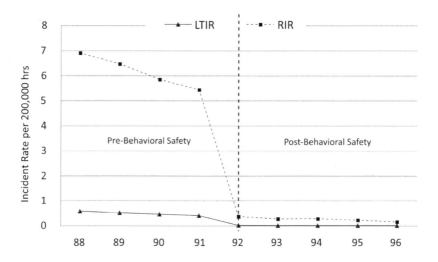

Exhibit 12.1: Cellophane- Before & After Recordable Incident Rates

Results

During the first year, the minor injury rate tumbled dramatically to 0.35, while Lost-time injuries reduced by a dramatic 82% to 0.01 per 200,000 hours worked! No lost-time accidents were recorded during or after the second year, while minor injuries showed a steady but consistent decline. In 1996, the site scooped the British Safety Councils highly prestigious 5 Star award.

Frozen Food Manufacturer

By 1995, McVities Frozen Foods had drastically improved its Health & Safety performance, to the extent that it was commonly recognized as the leader in the entire frozen foods business. Nonetheless, despite much effort, the site had reached a plateau and was finding it difficult to achieve their express aim of creating a Zero Incident Culture.

Although it was recognized that it is much more difficult to improve performance when safety standards are high, the results of audits and incident analysis, suggested that human factors and individual's behavior accounted for the performance plateau.

The Management Team looked at ways of introducing a step change that would bring about pro-active workforce involvement. They had come across Behavioral Safety by attending seminars, which promised workforce involvement while helping to breach the incident plateau. Visiting sites with Behavioral Safety processes and exploring the providers in the market, a workgroup based observation approach was preferred, as it would fit with the site's goal of establishing Self Directed Work Teams.

Assessment Survey

The process started with an assessment survey which revealed the company needed to make greater efforts to persuade the workforce that management were willing to adopt new ideas, invest the required time, money and effort to improve safety, become better informed about the safety problems related to people's jobs, and demonstrate that it cared about people's personal safety. They approached this by communicating to everybody that safety was the first item on the agenda at all management meetings; that line managers verbally communicate safety information to their workgroups, rather than just posting information on notice boards; involving the workforce in the safety decision-making process; and, senior management 'walking the talk' to specifically discuss safety issues with the workforce. As a whole, the survey results allowed the company to raise the profile of health and safety and immediately correct some of the shortfalls that were identified. As expected, this survey also revealed that many underlying issues were related to people's everyday safety behavior, which was at the core of the process adopted.

Workforce Briefings

Briefings were initially held with the senior management team in early 1996. These were very open, with the plan for Behavioral Safety fully discussed. The Factory General Manager then briefed the whole workforce of 410 people what the process was about and what the employee involvement would be. These briefings were conducted over a two day period, with each individual team, on each individual shift, inclusive of nights, back shifts, etc., each of which lasted for about an hour. The most significant thing that happened during these briefings was the stoppage of production, the first time ever that this had occurred at the site allowing employees to recognize the seriousness of the commitment given by all to be involved.

A need for three volunteer observers per shift for 11 work areas had been identified. The site actually recruited double the amount of volunteers, which proved to be extremely encouraging. Most of this was due to the fact that the open style of communication and the enthusiasm generated by all those involved up to this stage was seen as being infectious and everybody wanted to become involved.

Process Development

Six volunteers formed the B-Safe® project team, and over a five-day period they were taught to implement the Behavioral Safety process. The Team examined the incident records for the previous three years looking at total incidents, (i.e. all incidents that had occurred, to identify behaviors that were continually implicated in those incidents), so that the unsafe behaviors could be incorporated into each product areas observation checklist. From this process unsafe behaviors were identified and subsequently each incident was systematically examined to identify the relationship between the unsafe behavior and the work flow process. Importantly this allowed for the rectification of some oversights in risk assessments. It also proved useful for the B-Safe® Team to talk to the whole workforce as this led to the identification of further unsafe behaviors and activities that had not yet appeared in the incident records. These too were included on the Safety Behavior Checklists. In addition this provided an ideal opportunity for the B-Safe® Team to stimulate discussions and provide ongoing support to the whole of the workforce by explaining what the Behavioral Safety process was about and clarifying people's roles, while also being able to offer advice and any other explanations thought necessary.

Sixty-six volunteer observers were trained on a one-day course which was given by the leading coordinators within the B-Safe® Team. Prior to this, all middle management, (i.e. First Line Supervisors), were given a half-day session on the role of the volunteer observers. The main focus was on how these managers could help and support their observers to ensure a successful implementation. Following this training the observers completed a two-week practice period to ensure they were comfortable and conversant with their task. Moreover, the observers helped to further refine the observation checklists, with the full involvement of other employees. In practice, the process generated much enthusiasm, feedback, excitement and genuine commitment from everybody, who all wished to make the project succeed.

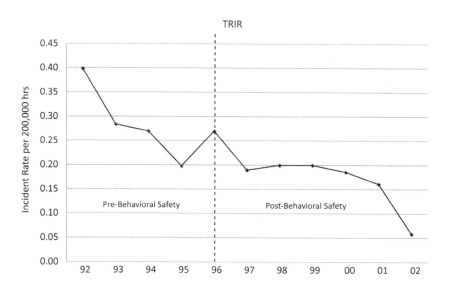

Exhibit 12.2: Frozen Foods- Before & After Incident Rates

Results

During the first six months safety behavior across the site improved by an average of 20 percentage points, from 73 percent to 93 percent. The checklist was then changed and new observers trained. At this time a baseline of 92 percent was scored, and over the next six months, the percent safe score achieved an average of 95 percent safe. This illustrates that the safer a facility becomes, the harder it also becomes to improve. In this first year, the recordable incident rate correspondingly fell by 29 percent, with the lost-time incident rate of Zero being achieved. By the end of 2002, the incident rate had reduced to 0.06 per 200,000 hours worked.

On the basis of the process and its results, the site's safety manager was awarded the safety professional of the year for the Food & Drinks industry, while the factory also received national honors and achieved a 20 percent reduction in its insurance premiums.

Long term Process Safety Results in a Petrochemical Site

Process Safety Management is currently a major issue in the Chemical, Oil & Gas and Petrochemical Industries after disasters such as Bhopal, BP Texas City, Esso Longford, Buncefield and numerous others. SABIC Petrochemicals (UK) Ltd has been addressing Process Safety management and people's safety behaviors since 1997 using Behavioral Safety as a primary mechanism.

SABIC's Olefins 6 (the cracker) is a single stream, high hazard, petrochemical installation of some 30 acres. The plant processes some 3million metric tons of hydrocarbon, mainly naphtha and propane and produces Olefins – Ethylene, Propylene and Butadiene as principal intermediate products. Derivates of these are used in the manufacture of a wide range of everyday household applications in use by us all, and a wide range of construction and engineering applications.

Because of the historical development of the Olefins business, storage and distribution of the cracker products is carried out on two additional locations on the same site, with a further riverside jetty for the handling of ships. The plant is operated continuously, with five to six years between major overhauls. It is manned by a team of 18 people per shift on a continuous shift pattern, with a further ten per shift in the storage and distribution areas.

In view of the hazards of the materials in use, safety is a paramount requirement. SABIC (previously ICI and Huntsman) started down the track of Behavioral Safety in 1997, on the cracker, on the back of eight years without a reportable injury (In the UK this is defined as serious injury such as amputation, broken bones, etc. or an incident resulting in a lost-time incident of more than three days). However the next most serious categorization of injury - recordable (one day lost-time), was showing an injury rate ranging between 5.5 and 0.75 per 200,000 hours, during the early 1990's. This varied in a cyclical fashion, with a slow improvement trend. People were getting hurt and the operations team had begun to realize that it was only a matter of time before someone would get hurt badly. It had been a matter of luck that one of the recordable injuries had not been much worse.   ·

Obtaining Buy-in

Management identified Behavioral Safety as a way forward, but recognized it would only work with 'shop floor' buy-in. The operations manager attended a Behavioral Safety workshop run by a well-known Behavioral Safety provider. This company conducted a formal assessment and presentations to the shift teams. The single biggest issue raised during this period, was about whether the process would actually make a difference to safety issues, or whether it would become a 'blame game'. Because the workforce was reluctant to adopt the process, the Union representatives and I were asked to talk with the shift teams on an informal basis. This resulted in them being persuaded to try it on a 'suck it and see' basis. At that time, two Behavioral Safety approaches were on offer: 'One-on-One, Peer-to-Peer' observations with a generic card from the well known company, or an employee-led workgroup based approach using specific checklists that I had implemented in other facilities (B-Safe®). The cracker shift personnel and the union representatives made the choice: they opted for the workgroup-based approach, as they perceived it to be less threatening. Site management also preferred this approach due to lower training requirements – from a cost and attendance time viewpoint, more flexibility in observation approaches, full training materials included in the package and overall lower costs. The shop floor also preferred it because it had a low overtime requirement for which they didn't get paid (the other method called for considerable amounts of overtime to complete the training).

Process Development

The project team consisted of a champion (the plant Operations Manager) and a full-time coordinator (a shift technician) who managed the project on a day-to-day basis. Beginning in November 1996, the plants previous incident records were examined by the consultants and the project coordinator to identify the small proportion of repeat behaviors triggering the majority of incidents. These were developed into a single checklist containing 20 specific behaviors to be used by all the shift teams that focused on Use of Tools, Access, Use of Hoses, Emergency Equipment, PPE and Housekeeping. The draft checklist was circulated to each shift and extensively discussed and refined by each workgroup until a final version was agreed.

Rollout and Execution

With the plant split into two areas (hot and cold end), 12 people (two from each of the shift teams) were trained as observers. Managers were also trained as observers so they could provide strong levels of support. After a four-week baseline period to establish current levels of performance, each workgroup set their own improvement target. Thereafter, each week's data was collated and analyzed, with tabulated reports presented at weekly team briefings. Using the Percent Safe score as the primary metric and daily observations, behavioral performance increased by 30 percent over the next 24 weeks.

The project champion also had provided the coordinator with a notional £100,000 annual improvement budget to be used to improve physical aspects of the plant that the shift teams thought were important. Numerous plant issues were identified. The coordinator collated these and then consulted with the shift teams to establish a priority for implementation. In this way the shift teams now had control of safety improvements that directly impacted upon their safety, within this budget. The coordinator also maintained this list, adding new items in as necessary and chasing the management team when they did not deliver the improvements within a reasonable timescale.

During this period, the cracker was shut down for a major six-week overhaul involving some 2500 contractor personnel. The Behavioral Safety process was adapted for this, and achieved excellent results. With almost double the amount of man-hours (550,000 Vs. 288,000), safety performance achieved a 50 percent reduction in the recordable incident rate, and a 100 percent reduction in reportable injury rates compared to the previous overhaul.

During the first six months, safety performance did not improve and in fact there were three recordable injuries. Two of these were thermal burns. One was caused by the failure of the shift team to fit a blank, as required by procedure. This led to a steam leak across a walkway that led to the inevitable injury. The second was caused by defective lagging on steam tracing. When setting up the second phase the teams could now see the impact of their behavior and their acceptance of sub-standard conditions. The new checklist included the observations for missing blanks and defective lagging (for example, 'all relevant hot and cold surfaces are lagged'). Thus the checklists moved from a 'pure' behavior checklist to a mix of behaviors and outcomes. During the baseline for phase 2, these new items were high scoring unsafe items and now the team could also see the value of setting improvement targets. This kick-started a massive improvement in the condition of the plant. Before B-Safe® the onus had been on the management team to carry out housekeeping audits to discover problems and the shift team saw defects as someone else's problem. Post B-Safe® the shift team took on the ownership of the condition of the plant. The operations manager simply had to ensure he could fund the remedial work within a reasonable timescale.

At the same time, the process was rolled out to Storage and Distribution and the Day Maintenance teams, following the exact same procedures described previously, except the baseline period was reduced to three weeks, which later was again reduced to two. These new groups also used mixed behavior and outcome checklists, containing very specific items. Behavioral Performance improved during this stage by around 30 percent, with Zero recordable injuries.

Based upon the observations made by the shift teams, where observations had been made of unsafe conditions, the coordinator either passed these back to the shift teams or the maintenance organization to remedy. He kept meticulous records and when remedial action was not taken within a reasonable timescale he chased the owning supervisor. In the early stages of implementation he had a number of problems with shift supervisors not giving these work lists adequate priority. He therefore asked the operations manager to educate these supervisors. It soon became apparent to these supervisors that on safety matters the coordinator acted with the delegated authority of the senior manager for the plant.

Another issue that came through 'loud and clear' at this time was the slow pace of major corrective action completion. This caused some observers to questions the process. They thought 'management' was only paying 'lip service' to safety. Examination of the corrective action system by the project coordinator identified a few 'blockages' in the support functions at the operational level in the incident causation chain (see chapter 4), illustrating how everyone within a company has an important part to play to achieve and maintain excellent safety performance. The blockages were rapidly dealt with by the Project Champion to ensure the execution of corrective actions was completed promptly. The systems subsequently set-up by the coordinator facilitated the measurement and tracking of the corrective actions to completion via a maintenance contractor network. This became the vehicle to involve the resident contractors in the process. By the end of 1999, 65 percent of personnel had been directly involved in the process as observers.

In 2000, using the same approach, the process began to include all the long-term resident contractors. By the end of 2001, the plant had achieved a Zero recordable incident rate, the first time ever in its history. Firmly focused on Process Safety Issues, during 2001, the plant observers identified 1400 unlagged hot and cold surfaces that were actioned by the project coordinator. Other issues highlighted and dealt with included, identifying and replacing 1431 short studs, replacing 1000 defective lights, renewing 150 pump plinth identification numbers, identifying 436 steam tracing / steam trap leaks with over 90 percent fixed, and the shift teams stenciling all 2472 Furnace burner identification numbers. Similar actions and quantities have been dealt with each and every year to help maintain the plant's integrity.

In 2002, the process was adapted once again for a major overhaul. With 495,000 man-hours worked, a Zero reportable injury rate was maintained and a further 25 percent reduction in recordable incidents. During 2003, the plant calculated the cost benefits at $500,000per year savings in steam leaks through identifying & making repairs. This reduction in energy consumption also directly reduced taxes incurred via the Climate Change Levy.   Additionally, insurance premiums reduced by 32 percent.

The process has continued to the present time and has been extended to other business units (e.g. Paraxylene, LDPE). In 2007, a review was held with the shift teams and some minor adjustments made to the process to maintain its sustainability. During, 2008, a further major overhaul with an excess of 1 million man-hours worked maintained the Zero reportable injury rate, and achieved its lowest ever recordable rate at 0.14.

Long-term results

It is difficult to quantify the exact impact that the Behavioral Safety process has had on plant integrity, but suffice to say, literally tens of thousands of physical plant issues have been attended to as a result of the behavioral observations. At the same time, the general levels of safety behavior have also improved significantly. The behavior changes are reflected in the long-term reduction in recordable incident rates shown in Exhibit 12.3.

After an initial surge during the first few months of operation, while the process became embedded, these show a continual downward trend that has removed the cyclical nature of the incident rate that was evident prior to Behavioral Safety. By and large, two-thirds of each checklist has targeted outcomes (i.e. plant integrity issues), and one-third behavior. Traditionally, Behavioral Safety checklists target 100 percent behavior. This case history shows that even with mixed types of checklist, it is possible to achieve both Zero incidents and improve Process Safety. The key to success is involving people in the improvement effort, supported by extremely strong managerial safety leadership, and an effective project team.

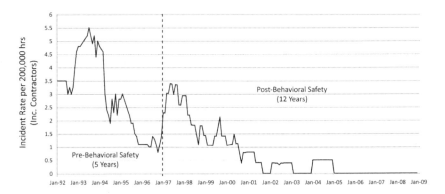

Exhibit 12.3: Petrochemicals -Before & After Recordable Incident Rates

Overall, by December 2008 in the United Kingdom, the combined SABIC businesses have achieved a Total Recordable Injury rate of 0.05, inclusive of resident contractors. Truly, everyone's actions have helped to achieve world-class performance.

Specialty Chemicals

Elementis Chromium employed 405 people to produce chromic acid and chrome sulfate for use in consumer products like automobile accessories, domestic appliances, plumbing fixtures, and hospital equipment. The site had experienced an annual climb in injuries over a five-year period that was considered unacceptable. People from the site visited local chemical sites operated by BASF, ICI and Norsk Hydro, recognized as leaders in safety performance in attempts to discover what they should be doing differently. All were giving prominence to Behavioral Safety processes. Elementis found that parts of each different process suited them, but not one was ideal. They then came across B-Safe® which was an employee-led process, visited sites implementing it, and decided that was the best way forward.

Obtaining Buy-in

In the fall of 1997, 70 percent of site employees (283 in total) attended a series of briefings about the process, in terms of what it intended to do, how it works and what it meant to them. A total of 35 volunteer observers were sought from the shift crews. Much to our delight, 86 volunteered.

Process Development

In March 1998 without conducting any form of assessment prior to starting, an employee representative was appointed as the full-time project coordinator and a senior manager took on the role of safety champion. Both received a week's training in their roles and duties. This included background information on behavioral principles, incident analysis, checklist development, observer training, goal setting, feedback, observation data-entry and analysis.

Examination of the sites incident records resulted in 14 separate checklists being developed containing general site categories (e.g. Housekeeping, PPE use, etc) and work area specific categories (hot surfaces & liquids, mobile plant, etc). These were distributed to all personnel for comment and discussed until a final agreement had been reached. The 86 volunteer observers and area 'team leaders' then each received one-days training in observation, feedback and coaching skills. They tested the observation checklists over a four-week period, which led to some revisions.

Rollout and Execution

The process began in earnest in the beginning of April 1998, when observers monitored their colleague's safety behavior at random times for 10-15 minutes per day, for a six-week period to establish an average baseline for each workgroup (i.e. how safely each workgroup was performing). This revealed that, as a whole, site personnel were behaving safely 62 percent of the time. Each workgroup was then asked to set their own safety improvement target, using the average baseline score for their workgroup. The site's average improvement target was set at 80 percent safe. Thereafter, the observers continued monitoring their workgroup's performance on a daily basis for a further 24 weeks. At the end of each week, every workgroup was provided with a printed analysis of their safety performance that was discussed at weekly 30-minute meetings. This provided each workgroup with relevant and timely feedback and the means to decide an action focus for the following week. This cycle of events was repeated every six months, with new behavioral checklists being developed and some 347 volunteer observers trained.

Integration with SMS

During the course of the project the employee coordinator was concerned to align the project with the site's existing safety management system. This was achieved by getting site personnel to risk assess problems that were found during the observations and the setting up of corrective action teams. Information was also passed on to improvement teams and safety committees. Similarly, 'live' safety topic boards were posted in each workgroup area. The spin-off benefits reported by the company include team ownership of safety standards; first and second line-management's ownership of safety; and a widely held belief in the company's commitment to safety. A further benefit was the gradual involvement of contractors in the observation process, which resulted in a 60 percent reduction in contractor incidents for the years 1999-2000.

Results

The results for improvements in levels of safety behavior and corresponding reductions in incidents are shown in Exhibit 12.4. During 1998 when the project went live, the site experienced 31 fewer incidents than in 1997. During 1999, 23 fewer incidents occurred than in 1998. In the year 2000, 49 fewer incidents occurred compared to 1999's figures. Overall since Behavioral Safety was introduced the company breached its incident plateau by approximately 66 percent. In 1999 through 2001 a Zero lost time incident rate was also achieved. The site was accredited to the International Occupational Health and Safety Management Standard - OSHAS 18001 - in October 2004.

In 2002, B-Safe® was rolled out to all the company's North American and UK operations. By 2008, this has helped the company reduce their

OSHA Total Recordable injury frequency rate by more than 70 percent.

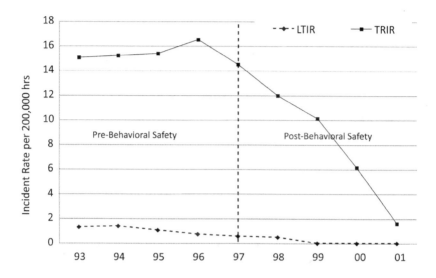

Exhibit 12.4: Specialty Chemicals - Before & After Incident Rates

Patient Safety

Adverse events in which harm is caused to patients is thought to cost the British National Health Service (NHS) an estimated £2 billion a year in additional hospital stays alone, without taking any account of human or wider economic costs. One of these adverse events is Hospital Acquired Infections (HAI). High profile British Government campaigns to reduce these, led the County Durham and North Tees Strategic Health Authority to trial Behavioral Safety in an Intensive Care unit in the James Cook University hospital in Middlesbrough.

In 2004, they had visited the local SABIC plant (see above) and thought Behavioral Safety techniques might help to reduce methicillin-resistant Staphylococcus aureus (MRSA) rates. Normal methods such as patient screening on admission, isolation of infected patients, staff training, barrier nursing, etc., had exerted some effects, but the rates were still considered to be too high. Illness attributable to MRSA is thought to increase intensive care unit stay by 8 days, hospital stay by 14 days, and the death rate by 35%. MRSA costs both the British and American health care systems billions of dollars a year in extended hospital stays, additional treatment costs and infection control costs.

Process Development

A team comprising of senior level Trust managers, the Behavioral Safety project team from SABIC and myself began with 'buy-in' sessions with the 140 doctors, nurses and care staff to brainstorm the behavioral issues. The idea was to engage staff in problem solving with regard to lack of resources, management systems, etc. and to try and identify the impact these exert on people's day-to-day behavior. For example, staff shortages often led to documentation being completed later in the shift, as staff dealt with another patients needs. Staff was informed that management would address the issues arising as quickly as was possible. To demonstrate management's commitment to improving quality care practices, many of the issues arising were actioned soon after the briefing sessions and then publicized. For example, a sink was placed just inside the ward by the entrance so that all visitors (i.e. doctors, nurses, staff and family) could wash their hands immediately upon entry to the ward.

A small project team was formed, starting with the Head of the Intensive Care Unit and the Clinical Matron as two 'Champions' from the management, their role being to provide leadership and motivation and ensure that time spent by others on the project was 'protected'. An ICU team member was appointed coordinator and trained in the basic principles and practice of the behavioral approach. This consisted of one day's training and several one-hour follow-up sessions on practical aspects and problems. Provided by SABIC's experienced Behavioral Safety coordinator, the training covered a six-stage process encompassing: [1] behavior analysis applied to incident records; [2] development of behavioral observation checklists; [3] observer training; [4] baseline establishment; [5] participative goal setting; and [6] feedback mechanisms. The one-hour follow up sessions concentrated on administration systems to facilitate tracking of the projects progress.

Front-line staff in a location or team – together with their line management – identified areas of concern they considered was needed to be successful as a group. Three of these were considered important and were categorized as [1] nursing documentation; [2] chart; and [3] hand washing. Within each category, specific behaviors (e.g., staff verbally instructing visiting teams to wash hands) or outcomes of behavior that needed to be performed to achieve the desired ends were identified. Outcomes of behavior (e.g. all entries delegated to others are countersigned by nurse) were used as proxies of behavior, as it could not be guaranteed that an observer would actually witness a nurse counter-signing during an observation. However, the observer could examine the documentation and assert whether this was being done or not. In this way, it could be determined whether or not staff was engaging in the desired behaviors. Thus the measures contained both behaviors and 'outcomes' of behavior.

The project team recruited and trained eight volunteer Health Care Assistants as observers. Each was trained how to observe, how to give verbal feedback and how to set participative improvement goals. They also visited the SABIC petrochemical plant to be given reassurance about the whole process by seeing it actually working. The observers monitored their colleagues in the wards for 10-20 minutes a day for one week, to establish a baseline. Each ward then set an improvement target. The health care assistants continued to monitor daily and gave feedback when observing people and at weekly feedback meetings. The project team followed up any corrective actions, the status of which was reported back to the workgroups. This cycle of events was repeated every 25 weeks or so.

Results

A steady improvement was recorded in all three categories of behavior over the next six months. As shown in Exhibit 12.5 MRSA rates reduced significantly by a stunning 70 percent. This degree of success equated to extra bed capacity value over $1,000,000 per annum. In November 2007 the Trust was named Britain's national *'Acute Healthcare Organization of the Year'* by the HSJ (Health Service Journal) at an award ceremony in London.

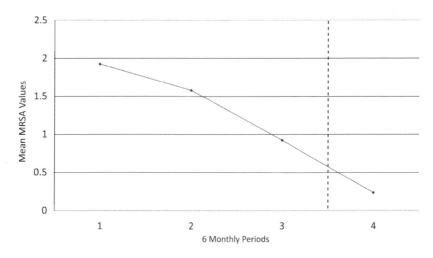

Exhibit 12.5: Mean MRSA Values Before & After Implementation

Construction of Two LNG Mega-Trains

A Joint Venture project comprising Chiyoda and Technip (CTJV) were awarded a turnkey Engineering, Procurement and Construction (EPC) contract for the construction of two 7.8Mta 'mega-trains' on behalf of RasGas, a Qatar Petroleum and ExxonMobil joint venture, in the State of Qatar. The overall scope of the project was immense involving major offshore and onshore construction, subsurface, drilling and engineering works. Involving 10 sub-contractors, and upwards of 45,000 people representing more than 60 different nationalities the initial stages of the construction project began in late 2005. The project comprised of building workers camps, common off plots with storage tanks, jetties, offshore pipeline and the construction of the two mega-trains.

To give an idea of the immense scale of the build, the main construction site was larger than 100 football fields put together. Train 6 alone used 200,000 tons of concrete, 45,000 tons of structural steel, 648 miles of piping, and over 3,107 miles of electrical cables (longer than a road trip from New York to Los Angeles!). In addition there were 200 cranes on site, with 250 buses to transport workers to and from their accommodation.

Background

With two consultants, we began implementing B-Safe® on the existing operating plant (OpCo) and the offshore platform in January 2006, where we held a series of Cultural Web Focus Groups exercises and briefings with the 2000 personnel workforce. A project coordinator was trained over five days. Plant specific safety checklists were developed and observers trained from resident contractors and plant personnel. Safety leadership checklists were also developed for senior, middle and front-line management. The project went live on a short three-week overhaul on Trains 1 and 2 at the end of March, where no injuries occurred at all. The process was then immediately rolled out on the plant, with checklists and observers changed every 4-5 months. By the end of 2008, almost 2.2 million observations had been conducted during 22 million man-hours worked, equating to an average 19,330 observations for every 200,000 hours worked.

Shown in Exhibit 12.6, in the past three years, incident rates have tumbled from an already low starting point. In 2006, the average TRIR decrease was 35 percent, followed by a further 21 and 58 percent in 2007 and 2008 respectively. The Lost time Incident Rate (LTIR) also tumbled by 62 percent in 2006, followed by further improvements of 23 and 45 percent in the following two years.

Construction Project Process Development

Once the process had started in the operating plant, attentions were turned to implementing the process on the construction project (RGX2). In May 2006 a project coordinator and champion from CTJV and four sub-contractors (i.e. Fluor, Q-Kentz, Dodsal and CCIC) were trained by the consultants. Each developed job specific checklists for their respective work activities. Many of these were translated into the 'mother tongues' of the workers (e.g. Nepali, Hindi). Senior, middle and front-line managers also developed safety leadership checklists. Further project coordinators were trained through August and September, from other sub-contractors arriving on site (i.e., Astaldi, ESS, Nasser Al Hajri, CBI, Teyseer and Medgulf). During this time, manpower was ramping up at a phenomenal rate (in some cases by over a 1000 people a week) to meet the tight production schedule.

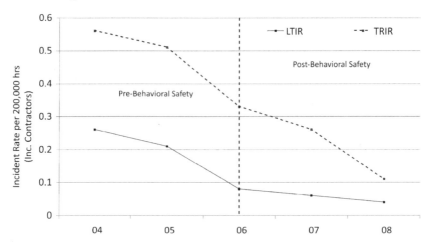

Exhibit 12.6: OpCo - Before & After Incident Rates

The project coordinators briefed everyone on site about the process as they arrived on site, and asked for volunteer observers. We aimed for a minimum two percent of the workforce being trained as observers to give a ratio of one observer to every 50 workers. Initially, this was a bit of a struggle, but within a week or two of gaining the workers trust, we were flooded with people wanting to be observers. These observers and many site safety officers were trained to observe, provide verbal feedback and coaching at one-day sessions.

Verbal feedback was provided at the point of observation and tabulated feedback sheets were discussed at 'tailgate' talks, with some sub-contractors doing this daily and others weekly. Monthly feedback sessions were also held amongst the various contractor coordinators to pass on innovations and to discuss any problems.

From a big picture viewpoint we monitored the various process metrics of all the sub-contractors to help keep the project on track. This included the numbers of personnel working on site, the ratio of observers to site personnel, the number of completed observations 'turned-in', the corrective action completion rate, the Percent Safe score, the Percent Safety Leadership score and the Visible Ongoing Support score.

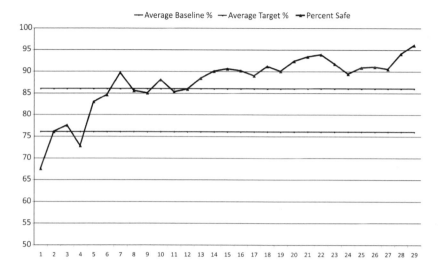

Exhibit 12.7: Construction- Combined Monthly % Safe Scores (2.5 Years)

Results

The project went live in July 2006. Over the next 25 months, with 239 million man-hours worked, 2.4 million safety observations were conducted, 321,000 safety leadership behaviors recorded, 121,000 VOS sheets completed by observers and more than 3900 corrective actions dealt with. Shown in Exhibit 12.7, combined levels of safety behavior across all the sub-contractors changed from an average of 76 Percent Safe at the project start to 96 Percent Safe by December 2008.

Despite the massive ramp-up of personnel numbers arriving on site the Lost-time Incident Rate consistently fell each year, by 20, 25 and 67 percent respectively (see Exhibit 12.8). There was an increase in recordable first-aid incidents in 2007 when manpower levels substantially ramped-up. The first week people are on a construction site is a classic time for them to get hurt as they become familiar with the site layout, activities and routines. Incident rates dropped back significantly in 2008.

In both 2007 and 2008, RasGas as a whole was recognized by the Oil & Gas Producers Association (OGP) and Shell Global Solutions (SGS), as the safest upstream Oil & Gas Company in the world.

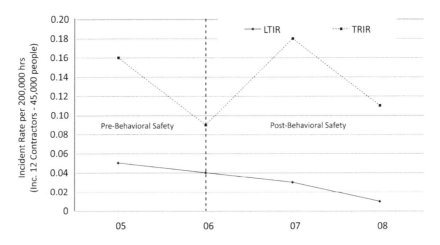

Exhibit 12.8: Construction - Pre and Post LTI and TRI rates

Summary

This small sample of case studies shows a consistent pattern of reducing injury rates using the workgroup-based approach with two-man project teams. In some instances, where there is a large workforce or site, separate project teams have been set-up. These teams then tend to meet monthly in order to keep abreast of developments in each area. By and large, this approach to Behavioral Safety resulted in an almost total elimination of injuries after about five years. Without a doubt, the benefits of a reduced likelihood of injury to personnel are considerable as well as injury cost savings, reductions in insurance premiums, and increased efficiencies. However, it takes a consistency of focus, purpose and execution. Behavioral Safety is not a 'wand' that can be waved to magically eliminate safety problems.

The average time taken to bring the incident rate down to 'world-class' levels of 0.05 per 200,000 hours worked are definitely a function of management's safety leadership and people's commitment to the process. In those facilities where a safety partnership has been created, *and* where the process continually targets incident triggering behaviors, much less time is taken and the results are more durable. Even then, the drive for continual improvement is never-ending.

Many facilities have gone years without experiencing any Lost-time incidents, then complacency has crept in and major catastrophes have occurred. This can be avoided by keeping on top of things by continually adapting the process. For example, by extending it to other important areas of activity, such as Process Safety, Ergonomics, Industrial Hygiene, Quality, Environment, etc., while also maintaining the focus on safety behavior. In this way, you keep people interested while continually refreshing the process. The business benefits will be huge.

Glossary of Terms

Assessment

A formal evaluation of the Behavioral, Cultural, System and Technical issues influencing people's safety behavior in a facility.

Baseline

Initial safety behavior performance level as measured based on the first few behavioral observations.

Behavioral Safety

Safety behavior improvement process 'that creates a *safety partnership* between management and the workforce by continually focusing everyone's attention and actions on their own, and others, safety behavior'.

Behavioral Safety Approach

Reflecting a company's fundamental underlying assumptions, a Behavioral Safety Approach can be supervisory-led (Top-down), Employee-led (bottom-up) or All-inclusive (Safety Partnership).

Behavioral Safety Maturity Ladder

An assessment tool comprising of a ladder that represents a continuum of Behavioral Safety approaches ranging from Beginning to Excelling. The higher up the ladder the more comprehensive the coverage, accountability and ownership.

Benchmarking

Comparison of safety assessment results against other companies (external) or other business units (internal).

Checklist

A checklist containing *specific* behaviors. These may be safety related, support-related or leadership related.

CLEAR

Acronym used to describe the overall implementation process that reflects Deming's 'plan, do, check, action' cycle.

Coaching

Joint exploration between observer and observed about how a job / task can be completed safely.

Corrective Action Rate

An indirect measure of management's commitment to safety. This is calculated by dividing the number of Corrective Actions completed, divided by the total number of Corrective Actions reported, and multiplying by 100 to produce a percent completed score.

Cultural Web   An assessment tool, comprising seven topics, used for Focus Group Exercises to identify, 'where are we now', 'where do we want to get to' and 'how are we going to get there'.

Data-Mining   A method used to identify the '*hidden patterns*' in incident databases, to ensure the process focuses on the small number of relevant behaviors involved in the majority of incidents.

Dynamic Settings   A work setting in a constant state of flux, resulting from transient workforces, or changing environments (e.g. construction).

Executive Sponsor   A member of the highest echelons of management who owns and sponsors the Behavioral Safety process.

Feedback   Information received about ongoing behavioral performance. Can be verbal, graphical, or tabulated.

Feedback Report   Tabulated observation data highlighting summary observation scores and the top 3-5 best / worst scoring behaviors, specific to a group of people. Usually, presented at weekly feedback meetings to workgroups. Sometimes used by steering committees to obtain overview of progress on monthly basis.

Focus Groups   A mechanism that focuses on particular issues to identity resolutions to problems.

Generic Checklist   A checklist that contains generic categories of behavior (e.g. housekeeping, access, etc), but containing specific behaviors in each category.

Goal-Setting   The process where workgroups set themselves improvement targets on the basis of baseline behavioral observations. Workgroups track their progress against these targets on a weekly basis.

IDEAL   An acronym used to describe the Behavioral Safety implementation stages.

Improvement Targets   A motivational mechanism for obtaining commitment to raising the standards of safety and other behaviors.

Involvement   People's participation in the design and execution of the Behavioral Safety process.

Job-Specific Checklist   A checklist for a particular task or job containing specific behaviors to improve.

Key Performance Indicators   Indicators to measure progress that are often expressed in percentages. These include Corrective Action Rates, Participation Rates, Observation Rates, Percent Safe Scores, Safety Leadership Scores, and Visible Ongoing Support Scores.

Key Principles   Ethical guides for how a Behavioral Safety process will be implemented and run.

Kick-off meeting   A meeting held with the workforce to announce the Behavioral Safety process has gone 'live' with checklists developed and being used by observers on the ground.

Managerial Safety Leadership Checklist   A checklist of managerial behaviors (sometimes divided into 4 categories - people, system, training & observer support) developed by each management team that is used to track managements visible and demonstrable safety leadership, at senior, middle and front-line levels.

Observers   Generally, people who make behavioral observations using observation checklists to guide them.

Observation   The act of observing behavior and recording the findings on any checklist type. Observations can be 'one-on-one', workgroup-based or self-managed.

Observation Card   A 'generic' card containing multiple categories that tries to cover every aspect of people's safety behavior.

Observation Rate   The number of observations completed, divided by the number expected, multiplied by 100.

Operational Definitions   A list of numerous behavior types that is often used to support a generic observation card, to help guide observers when conducting observations.

Outcome Based Checklist — Generally, a checklist focused on the outcomes of behavior (e.g. hoses across walkways). Often used in facilities where it is difficult to observe people because they are few in number (e.g. chemical plants). Sometimes used to improve Process Safety by focusing on plant integrity issues.

Participation Rate — The number of people actively observing, compared to the number trained to observe, multiplied by 100.

Percent Safe Score — Essentially the ratio between safe and unsafe behaviors. Calculated by totaling the number of safe behaviors observed, dividing by the total number of behaviors observed and multiplying by 100 to produce a Percent Safe score.

Percent Safety Leadership Score — The number of safety leadership behaviors completed, divided by the total number expected, multiplied by 100.

Project Team — Usually a two-person team who directs and runs entire Behavioral Safety process, instead of a steering committee.

Project Champion — Senior manager who provides the necessary leadership and direction, by being visible, 'walking the walk' and 'talking the talk'. Usually reports on progress to senior management teams. Essentially, a persuader, troubleshooter, problem solver and motivator.

Project Coordinator — Full-time person(s) dedicated to overseeing the implementation, data collection, and processing of behavioral observations and provider(s) of feedback to the workgroups and senior management teams.

Reviews — Formal evaluations to ensure process sustainability

Rollout and Execution — Refers to the active implementation of the Behavioral Safety plan.

Scorecards — Cards containing Key Performance Indicators to monitor and assess Behavioral Safety progress.

Static Setting — A work- setting in a constant stable state, with a fixed workforce, and production processes.

Steering Committee	A part-time group of 7-12 people devoted to planning, implementing and running a Behavioral Safety process.
Strategic Roadmap	A visual 'aide memoir' developed and used for planning multiple site, or large scale corporate implementations.
Task Force	Usually a group of people charged with the day to day rollout of large scale corporate implementations.
'Tell & Sell' Briefing	Initial briefing to all personnel outlining the Behavioral Safety process to obtain 'buy-in'.
Visible Ongoing Support	A checklist completed weekly that employee observers use to indicate the amount of management support they have received.
Weekly Briefing	Usually a 30 minute meeting where a workgroup discuss the tabulated results of the previous weeks observations.
Workgroup's Weekly Observation Feedback Report	A tabulated analysis of a workgroups observation results for the previous week, that contain Percent Safe results by category and highlights the top 5 safe and unsafe behaviors performed.

References

Adams, E. (1976). Accident Causation & the Management Systems. *Professional Safety,* Oct, (ASSE).

Atkinson, P.E. (1990). *Creating Culture Change: The Key to Successful Total Quality Management.* IFS Publications, Kempston.

Autry, J.A. (2004). *The Servant Leader: How to Build a Creative Team, Develop Great Morale, and Improve Bottom-Line Performance.* Three Rivers Press. NY.

Bandura, A. (1986) *Social Foundations of Thought and Action: A Social Cognitive Theory.* Englewood Cliffs, NJ: Prentice-Hall.

Bird, Jr. F. E., (1974) *Management Guide to Loss Control.* Atlanta: Institute Press.

Chandler, B. and Huntebrinker, T.A. (2003). Multisite Success with Systematic BBS: A Case Study. *Professional Safety.* June. 35-42.

Cooper, J.O., Heron, T.E., & Heward, W.L. (1987). *Applied Behavior Analysis.* Columbus. OH: Merrill Publishing Co.

Cooper, M.D. (1998). *Improving Safety Culture: A Practical Guide.* J Wiley & Sons.

Cooper, M.D. (2000). Towards a Model of Safety Culture. *Safety Science,* 32, 111-136.

Cooper, M.D. (2001). Treating Safety as a Value. *Professional Safety,* 46, 17-21.

Cooper, M.D. (2002). Understanding and Quantifying Safety Culture: A reciprocal model for success. *Professional Safety,* 47 (6), 30-36.

Cooper, M.D. (2003). Psychology, Safety and Risk. *Professional Safety,* 48 (11), 39-46.

Cooper, M.D. (2003). Behavior-Based Safety Still A Viable Strategy. *Safety & Health,* National Safety Council, April. 46 – 48.

Cooper, M.D. (2005). Work Motivation. *In: Tim Hannagan (Ed) 'Management: Concepts & Practices' (4th Ed).* FT Prentice Hall: London.

Cooper, M.D. (2006). The Impact of Management's Commitment on Employee Behavior: A Field Study. *American Society of Safety Engineers Middle East Chapter, Proceedings of the 7th Professional Development Conference & Exhibition,* Kingdom of Bahrain, 40-47.

Cooper, M.D. (2006). Exploratory analysis of the effects of managerial support and feedback consequences on Behavioral Safety maintenance, *Journal of Organizational Behavior,* 26(3), 1-41.

Cooper, M.D. (2007). Behavioral -Safety User Survey Report. www.behavioral-safety.com.

Cooper, M. D. (2008). Risk-Weighted Safety Culture Profiling. *SPE International Conference on Health, Safety, Security & Environment in Oil & Gas Exploration and Production.* 15-17 April 2008, Nice, France.

Cooper, M.D. (2009). Behavioral Safety Interventions: A review of process design factors. *Professional Safety,* 54, 36-45.

Cooper, M.D. & Phillips, R.A. (2004). Exploratory analysis of the safety climate and safety behavior relationship. *Journal of Safety Research,* 35, 497 – 512.

Cooper, M.D., Phillips, R.A., Sutherland, V.J., and Makin, P.J., (1994). Reducing Accidents with Goal-Setting and Feedback: A Field Study. *Journal of Occupational and Organizational Psychology.* 67, 219-240.

Cooper, M.D., Farmery, K., Johnson, M., Harper, C., Clarke, F.L., Holton, P., Wilson, S., Rayson, P., and Bence, H. (2005). Changing personnel behavior to promote quality care practices in an intensive care unit. *Therapeutics and Clinical Risk Management;* 1(4): 321–332.

Daniels, A. & Daniels, J.E. (2004). Performance Management: Changing Behavior that Drives Organizational Effectiveness. PMP, Georgia.

DePasquale, J.P & Geller, E.S. (1999). Critical Success Factors for Behavior-Based Safety: A Study of Twenty Industry-wide Applications. *Journal of Safety Research*, 30, 237-249.

Douglas, T.J. & Judge, W.Q. (2001). Total Quality Management Implementation and Competitive Advantage: The Role of Structural Control and Exploration. *The Academy of Management Journal*, 44, 158-169.

Duff, A.R., Robertson, I.T., Cooper, M.D., & Phillips, R.A., (1993). Improving Safety on Construction Sites by Changing Personnel Behavior. *HMSO Report Series CRR 51/93*: HMSO London.

Federal Railroad Administration. (2007). Behavior-Based Safety at Amtrak-Chicago Associated with Reduced Injuries and Costs.

Geller, S. (1998). *The Psychology of Safety: How to improve behaviors on the job*. CRC Press: Boca Raton.

Greve, H.R. (2003). *Organizational learning from performance feedback: a behavioral perspective on innovation and change*. Cambridge University Press.

Grindle, A. C., Dickinson, A. M., & Boettecher, W. (2000). Behavioral Safety and Research in Manufacturing Settings: A Review of the Literature. *Journal of Organizational Behavior Management*, 20, 29– 68.

Health & Safety Executive. (2003). Huntsman Petrochemicals. Case Studies- Large businesses. www.hse.gov.uk.

Heinrich, H.W., Peterson D., & Roos N. (1980). *Industrial Accident Prevention* McGraw-Hill, New York.

Howe, J. (1998). A Union Critique of Behavior Safety. *Orlando, FL. UAW, International Union*.

Kirwan, B. and Ainsworth, L. (Eds.) (1992). *A guide to task analysis*. Taylor and Francis.

Krause, T.R. (1995). *Employee-Driven Systems for Safe behavior: Integrating Behavioral and Statistical Methodologies*. Von Nostrand Reinhold.

Krause, T.R, Seymour, K.J. & Sloat, K.C.M (1999). Long-term evaluation of a behavior-based method for improving safety performance: a meta-analysis of 73 interrupted time-series replications. *Safety Science*, 32, 1-18.

Leigh, P.J. (2008). Costs of Occupational Injury and Illness Combining All Industries. Seminar for Western Center for Agriculture Health and Safety, University of California, Davis, CA.

Linderman, K., Schroeder, R.G., Zaheer, S., Choo, A.S. (2003). Six Sigma: a goal-theoretic perspective. *Journal of Operations Management* 21, 193–203.

Locke, E.A. & Latham, G.P. (1990). *A Theory of Goal Setting and Task Performance*. Prentice-Hall.

McSween, T. E. (2003). *The Values-Based Safety Process*. Wiley Inter-Science. NJ.

Mattilla, M., Rantanen, E., & Hyttinen, M. (1994). The quality of supervision and safety work environment in building construction. *Safety Science, 17,* 257-268.

Marsh, T.W., Davies, R., Phillips, R.A., Duff, A.R., Robertson, I.T., Weyman, A., & Cooper, M.D. (1998). The Role of Management Commitment in Determining the Success of a Behavioral Safety Intervention. *Journal of the Institution of Occupational Safety & Health, 2,* 45-56.

OGP. (2009). Safety Performance Indicators – 2008 data. Report 419, May.

Olsen, R., and Austin, J. (2001). ABC's for Lone Workers: A Behavior-Based Study of Bus Drivers. *Professional Safety*. Nov. 20-25.

Pate-Cornell, M.E. (1992). *A post-mortem analysis of the Piper-Alpha accident: Technical and Organizational Factors*. Research Report No. 92-2, Management of Human Error in Operations in Marine Systems Project. Department of Naval Architecture and Offshore Engineering, University of California at Berkeley.

Pounds, J. (2009). Seven Reasons Why Your Behavior-based Safety Process is Flopping. May 21. http://bbsfoundations.com.

RasGas. (2009). Celebrating Safety Achievements. *RasGas Magazine*, 25, pp 3 and 7.

Real, K., & Cooper, M.D. (In Press) Communication climate as a determinant of safety climate, *Safety Science*.

Reason J. (1997). Managing the Risks of Organizational Accidents *Ashgate, Aldershot, Hants*.

Reber, R. A., & Wallin, J. A. (1984). The effects of training, goal setting, and knowledge of results on safe behavior: A component analysis. *Academy of Management Journal, 27*, 544-560.

Rechenthin, D. (2004). Project Safety as a Sustainable Competitive Advantage. *Journal of Safety Research, 35*, 297-308.

Robertson, I.T., Duff, A.R., Marsh, T.W., Phillips, R.A., Weyman, A. & Cooper, M.D. (1999). *Improving Safety on Construction Sites by Changing Personnel Behavior (Phase 2)*. Health & Safety Executive: HSE Books.

Saari, J. & Naesaenan, M. (1989). The effect of positive feedback on industrial housekeeping and accidents: A long-term study at a shipyard. *International Journal of Industrial Ergonomics, 4*, 201-211.

Seddon, J. (1989). *'A passion for quality'*, The TQM Magazine, May, pp. 153-7.

Staff. 'How Does Behavioral Safety work?' Cambridge Center for Behavior Studies.

Stewart, D.A. & Townsend, A. S. (1999). Is there more to 'Health & Safety is Good Business' than avoiding unplanned costs. *www.behavioral-safety.com/articles*.

Sulzer-Azaroff, B. and Austin, J. (2000). Does BBS Work? Behavior-Based Safety and Injury Reduction: A Survey of the Evidence. *Professional Safety*, July, 19-24.

Walker, S. (2008). Effective Implementation of Behavior-Based Safety in the Unique Petroleum Industry. *SPE International Conference on Health, Safety, and Environment in Oil and Gas Exploration and Production*, 15-17 April 2008, Nice, France.

Walton, M. (1986). *The Deming Management Method*. Perigee, N.Y.

Weaver, D. (1971). Symptoms of Operational Error. *Professional Safety*, Oct (ASSE).

Wirth, O. & Sigurdsson, S.O. (2008). When workplace safety depends on behavior change: Topics for Behavioral Safety research. *Journal of Safety Research, 39*, 589–598.

Wilkinson, A., Allen, P., & Snape, E. (1991). TQM and the management of labor. *Employee Relations, 13*, 24-31.

Index